Learn Spanish
for Everyone

How to Understand and Speak

Spanish Grammar with Phrases,

Exercises and Pronunciation.

Ray Moreno

Table of Contents

INTRODUCTION 6

    A.   METHOD OF LEARNING A NEW LANGUAGE 7
    B.   THE SPANISH LANGUAGE 7
    C.   HOW TO PRONOUNCE THE VOWELS 9
    D.   PRONUNCIATION..9
    E.   WHERE TO GO FROM HERE 14
    F.   THE STRESS RULES..14

BUSINESS 16

    SALIENDO A COMER (EATING OUT).............................16
    MAKING A RESTAURANT RESERVATION 23
    MAKING A RESTAURANT ORDER..............................25
    AT THE RESTAURANT 28
    SPANISH CELEBRATIONS 31
    VIAJAR (TRAVEL) 33
    EL TRANSPORTE / TRANSPORTATION 40
    SHOPPING 42
    EL DINERO (MONEY)...48
    EL TRABAJO (WORK, JOB) 49

HOBBIES & STUDY SITUATIONS 51

    HOBBIES 51
    STUDIES SITUATIONS 52

BASIC VOCABULARY 57

IDIOMS, SAYINGS, MODISMS & PROVERBS 92

EASY SPANISH PHRASES 102

    TRANSPORT 102
    TRAVEL 106
    SHOPPING 108

CONCLUSION... 116

(CONCLUSIÓN).. 116

Introduction

Are you one of those people who have been considering learning a new language? Is Spanish the one you are considering to learn?
In case you didn't know yet, Spanish is one of the most widely spoken languages in the world. More than five hundred million individuals are native Spanish speakers. Therefore, by that figure, it is considered as the second most sought-after language following Mandarin Chinese. Apart from that, a study has shown that it's the most romantic of all languages. No matter if you wish to learn the language simply to widen your knowledge or you simply want to learn it because you're traveling a Spanish-speaking destination, you will require a guide to make your whole learning process much simpler and stress-free.

This book is suitable for you, especially if you're not trying to pass a Spanish class. That's because it will get you speaking the language quick. In any scenario, you don't need to be a language professor just to speak the language. This book will surely teach you how to speak the language with the help of simple and practical examples. It will also walk you through discussions to help you get your point across whenever you are meeting new individuals, finding directions, going shopping, traveling, eating in a restaurant, and so much more. In short, this book will guide you on how to speak Spanish virtually in any sort of situation.

The good thing here is that you won't find boring grammar lessons and rules you wouldn't bother with anyway. As an alternative, you will explore many practical examples as well as notes, which will guide you on how to understand better how to speak. While the Spanish language isn't as complex to learn as English is, the language does have its quirks, you must be familiar. You will find many reasons for desiring to learn the Spanish language. First, because being bilanguage will make you desirable in the job marketplace. It will also provide you a higher sense of self-confidence if you could step in and assist individuals who are having a difficult time with the language barrier out in public. Have you ever thought of how many instances you've seen somebody speaking the language and having trouble to communicate with other people? You wish you could help them but you can't. Today, you don't need just to stand there. You could finally step in and help both people. Learning a new language like Spanish is advantageous to your self-value and resume as well. What's more, it is a wonderful way to keep your brain exercising. Some people don't stop learning. Therefore, learning a new language could be your initial step to continuing education.

As you now go on along with the learning journey, you'll discover different vital tips, which make will understanding and speaking the language much simple. Using this book, you could be talking Spanish in no time at all. Best of luck and buen viaje!

A.   Method of Learning a New Language

Efficient language learners have a positive response when faced with the unfamiliar. Therefore, instead of letting yourself to feel pissed, confused, and frustrated every time listening to Spanish, why don't you try to keep a positive point of view? Start working to know anything you could. It could help you think of speaking in Spanish as a puzzle to be solved, or it could be an interesting challenge to be reached. Every time you hear spoken Spanish, you must concentrate on what is being told. Do not get distracted by your negative ideas. Listen for cognates that are words, which are similar or almost the same in two languages. Take note that English and Spanish share many cognates. Some of these are much / **mucho**; culture / **cultura**; aspect / **aspecto**; important / **importante**; professor / **professor**; introductory / **introductorio**; and course / **curso**.

B.   The Spanish Language

The Spanish language is also called as **castellano** or **español.** This language was established in the Iberian Peninsula in the region of Castile. Spanish is considered as the third most spoken language in the world, according to the United Nations. Approximately, at least half a billion of folks speak the language. It is spoken on four continents and is the official language of twenty nations.

Aside from that, the language is also spoken more every year in the mainland of the U.S. In fact, approximately forty million individuals in the U.S. speak the language at home. That makes up over twelve percent of the population of the country. A 2015 report conducted by a government organization in Spain sowed that there are more Spanish speakers in the U.S. compared there to Spain.

You will find three major differences, which determine how this language is spoken in one region versus another. This includes grammar, accent, and vocabulary. The differences in vocabulary lead in various words utilized in various locations to refer to a similar thing. For instance, the word "the computer" in Latin America is **la computadora**. Meanwhile, you will say it in Spain as **el ordenador**.

When we talk about the accent, you will find some variances among regions. You will also find differences between regions in a similar country. The most evident difference in accent among those Spanish speaker connects to the way to say the letter **z**, the letter **c** then followed by **e** or **i**.

Another example is in Latin America, the letter **z, as well as the letter,** mixes **ci** and **ce** are spoken along with an **s** sound. On the other hand, in central and northern Spain, it was spoken along with **th** sound. For instance, the term for "shoe" is **zapato**. In Latin America, it is uttered as **sapato.** In Madrid, it is spoken as **thapato.**

You might not notice many grammatical differences among regions. However, there are some, which deal with the plural form of "you." In both Latin America and Spain, the term **ustedes** is the formal and plural way to talk "you." Meanwhile in Spain, you will find an informal and plural way to utter "you." **Vosotras** in the feminine while **vosotros** in the masculine. However, **vosotras** and **vosotros** aren't utilized in Latin America. As an alternative, **ustedes** is utilized for the plural "you" in every scenario. Regardless of such differences in grammar, accent as well as vocabulary, thousands of Spanish speakers converse efficiently across every region where the language is pronounced. Even those speakers of Spanish from various countries understand one another totally well.

C. How to Pronounce the Vowels

Speaking words in Spanish is easier than it is in the English language. That's mainly because if you see a letter in Spanish, you will understand how to speak the sound of that particular letter. The only difficult part of the pronunciation of the Spanish language is that you will find sounds in the language, which do not exist, in the English language. All of them could be hard to speak at first.

Every vowel – **a, e, i, o, u** – make only one sound in Spanish. It is only a quick sound, which remains the same from start to finish,

Here's a detailed example:

- The vowel **A** seen in the typical Spanish term **casa** is the simplest vowel sound to create. The other four vowel sounds concentrate on maintaining the vowel sound brief and constant.
- The vowel **E** creates the sound spoken in the English word "take." You see, it is not pronounced "eyyyy." You do not end it off at the end as we mostly do in the English language.
- The vowel **I** create the sound spoken in the word "fee." It is not "iyyy."
- The vowel **B** creates the sound spoken in "toil." It is not "owww."
- The vowel **U** creates the sound spoken in "rule." It is not "uwww."

D. Pronunciation

Pronunciation is vital in any type of language. Therefore, get the hang of this before you try to talk to someone. Nowadays, it is much simpler, simply because you will find countless videos online that will aid you. In this section, you will learn how to utter individual letters by fitting them into typical, easily spoken Spanish words.

One benefits of Spanish over the English language is that with the majority of words, the pronunciation is phonetic. You see, the words sound as if they're spelled. You will also find some homophones that will puzzle you. Some of those words include "they're," "their," and "there" that sound the same;

however, have different spellings and meanings. Below is a brief guide to Spanish pronunciation.

The Vowels

In the Spanish language, you will find five vowels and one sound for every vowel.

[a]	ah	The 'a' is spoken as if you were gargling. Simply open your mouth wide and say as saw and father. Try **mapa, agua.**
[e]	eh	The 'e' sound isn't totally existent in English. The nearest pronunciation might be 'eh' as red and met. You must not say the 'e' as in English. You can try saying **enero**, **verde.**
[i]	ee	The 'i' sound is somewhat similar to 'ee' as bee and feet. You see, the 'i' sound is much different compared to the English pronunciation. For instance, **mi, fino.**
[o]	oh	The letter 'o' is uttered as 'oh.' However, it has a shorter sound as know and boat. You can try **roto, coco.**
[u]	oo	This is pronounced as 'oo' like in do or boot. Try saying **muro**, **futuro.**

The Diphthongs

In case you didn't know yet, a diphthong is a sound that was made by a mix of two (2) vowels in a single syllable. A sound starts as one vowel and moves to another.

$	a	+	i	$	ai, ay	The 'ai' and 'ay' sound is like ay and why. You can try speaking **mayo, aire.**
$	a	+	u	$	au	The 'au' sounds like the expression auch. You can try speaking **aula, aunque.**
$	e	+	u	$	eu	You will not find a sound for this in the English language. That was something like ew however, with

		the use of the 'e' sound as bed and the 'u' as do. You can try saying **deudor, Europa.**
|e|+|i|	ey, ei	The pronunciation of 'ey' and ei' is near to say and hey. Try saying **buy, reina.**
|i|+|a|	ia	The 'ia' will sounds like tiara and yah. Try saying **anciano, piano.**
|i|+|e|	ie	The 'ie' sounds similar to yes. Try saying **fiera, tierra.**
|i|+|o|	io	The 'io' is uttered as John or yo-yo. Try saying **rio, radio.**
|i|+|u|	iu	The 'iu' is uttered as you. You can try saying **viuda, ciudad.**
|o|+|i|	oy, oi	The 'oy' and 'oi' sounds similar to boy and toy. Try saying **heroico, hoy.**
|u|+|a|	ua	The 'ua' sound is similar to water. You can try saying **aduana, actuar.**
|u|+|e|	ue	The 'ue' sounds similar to wet. Try saying **sueńo** and **Huevo**.
u|+|i|	ui	The 'ui' sounds is similar to wheat and we. Try saying **huir, arruinar.**
|u|+|o|	uo	The 'uo' sounds similar to continuous and quote. Try saying **cuota, individuo.**

The Consonants

A series of Spanish consonants are pronounced differently from their English counterparts. If you could, you can try to listen to a local speaker and hear how they deal with them.

[b]	Beh	The letter 'b' is uttered after n, m, or l. The sound of this letter is similar to bear and Venice, even though the lips should not touch. For example, **bonito.**
[c]	Ceh	The letter 'c' sounds like cereal before i or e. Or else, it might sound like 'k' as computer. For example, **computadora** as 'k' and **cereza** as 'c.'
[ch]	Cheh	For example, **chico, chocolate.**

[d]	Deh	For example, **dos, dust.**
[f]	Effe	The letter 'f' sounds similar in the English fountain or Eiffel. For example, **familia.**
[g]	Heh	The 'g' sounds is similar to her before i or e. Or else, it sounds like get or got. For example, **guante** as 'get,' **gesto** as 'her.'
[h]	Hache	The letter 'h' in Spanish is silent. For example, **hilo.**
[j]	Hotah	The letter 'j' sounds harsh or horse. But never as jump or jar. For example, **jirafa.**
[k]	Kah	The letter 'k' sounds similar as in the English language. It is pronounced as key or car. For example, **koala.**
[l]	Ele	The letter 'l' is uttered as like or lord. For example, **lobo.**
[ll]	double ele, elle	The double 'l' is spoken as the 'y' in yesterday. For example, **calle.**
[m]	Emeh	The letter 'm' is similar as in the English man or mother. For example, **modo.**
[n]	Eneh	The letter 'n' sounds similar as in the English note and no. For example, **nosotros.**
[ń|	Enyeh	The 'ń' isn't another letter 'n'. This letter sounds as canyon, onion or lasagna. For example, **nińa.**
[p]	Peh	The letter 'p' is similar to the sound in the English paste or pet. For example, **pelo.**
[q]	Koo	The letter 'q' is spoken as curious. If it is written with 'ue' and 'ui' the letter 'u' is silent. For instance, '¿quién?' is spoken as *kien.* What's more, the '¿qué?' as *ke* (using the Spanish 'e'). For example, **qué, quién**.
[r]	Ere	The letter 'r' sounds like brr at the start of a word. Or else, it sounds like brown or break. For example, **raton** as 'brr,' **crear** as 'break.'

[rr]	Erre	The double 'r' sounds like 'r' at the start of a word. It is sound is much vibrated, as the sound of a vehicle accelerating. For example, **perro.**
[s]	ese	The letter 's' sounds similarly as in the English language sea or sorry. For example, **solo.**
[sh]	esse / hache	The 'sh' sounds as show or shampoo. For example, **show.**
[t]	teh	The 't' sound is pronounced as in English, even though the tongue needs to touch the back of your teeth like test and tea. For example, **tela.**
[v]	veh	The 'v' sounds are proncounced as the letter 'b.' However, your lips are touched slightly as voice or various. For example, **vecino.**
[w]	doble veh	The 'w' sounds have a similar pronunciation as in the English language wine and whiskey. For example, **kiwi.**
[x]	equis	The 'x' sound is spoken as 'gs' or 'ks' like in excited or explosion. For example, **xilófono**.
[y]	i griega / ye	The letter 'y' is the same as the double 'l.' However, it has a slight difference as yellow and crayon. For example, **yegua.**
[z]	Setah	The letter 'z' is uttered as 'th' not as in zero or zip. For example, **zorro.**

Are you now looking for ways to make it simpler for you to say these letters as a native Spanish speaker? Then there's no need for you to worry. You could look online for an audio file and listen to it to make sure you get it all right. We suggest that you stay away from any translation software when learning how to pronounce any word in the Spanish language. The reason behind this is that such applications do not have the required accent to make you pronounce each word accurately.

Make sure you look for real individuals speaking in the native Spanish language on different video platforms. These people tend to speak authentic Spanish, meaning you could learn more from them and much quicker.

E. Where to Go From Here

The best thing about this book is that you don't need to read them every chapter from the start to the end. Every chapter stands on its own, and it does not oblige you to finish any other of the chapters within the book. That setup saves you sufficient time if you have mastered particular topics but feel somewhat insecure about the others.

Therefore, make sure you leap right in. Now is a perfect time that you get your feet wet. If you not certain exactly where to start, you can look at the Table of Contents. Choose the topic, which appears to best suit your requirements and capabilities. If you are getting concerned that your existing background might not be strong enough, you could begin at the very start. From them, you could work way throughout the book.

Just bear in mind that learning the Spanish language is not a sort of competition. You must work at a pace, which fits your needs. Do not pause to read a chapter a second, third, or even fifth time many days later. Take note that you could adapt this book easily into your learning skills. You need to take note that you should have a positive and confident outlook towards this. Indeed, you will make some mistakes. Everybody does – in fact; most native Spanish speakers always do. Your goal here is to speak and write. If you could make yourself understood, you have won the greatest part of the war.

F. The Stress Rules

You are already aware that Spanish words are stressed on the *last syllable* when they end in a consonant other than s or n. For example, **Gibraltar, Santander, El Escorial, Valladolild.**

You see, they are stressed on the *syllable before last* when they end in s or n or a vowel. For example, **Valdepeñas, Toledo, Granada.**

When a particular word breaks either of such rules, an accent is written to highlight where the stress falls. For example, **civilización, José, Gifón, kilómetro, Cádiz, Málaga.** Every word ending in –ion bears that accent. Therefore, if you notice a written accent, you should stress the syllable where the accent is located. The only other usage of accents you must understand is that it is situated on *si* to distinguish **si** (yes) from **si** (if).

The only other usage of accents you must understand is that it is situated on *si* to distinguish **si** (yes) from **si** (if).

Business

SALIENDO A COMER (EATING OUT)

When it comes to food, every culture always has something to showcase. It has become an important element of every culture. When it comes to tasting the food, restaurant hopping and trying new dishes, Latin America has the most diverse offerings. For specifics, deep-dried fish, mountain-cured ham and a variety of other treats are waiting for you in Spain.

In this chapter, you will be introduced to having the table talk so you can be able to order food on your own at the recommended restaurants and shop for food at the market, with the confidence that you will get exactly what you want.

First off, here are some meal terminologies:

desayuno (m) - breakfast

comida (f) - lunch

cena (f) - dinner

tentempié (m) - snack

comer - eat

beber - drink

Por favor. - Please.

Quisiera ... - I'd like ...

¡Estoy hambriento/a! (m/f) - I'm starving!

tengo sed - I'm thirsty

TABLE TERMS

When you are planning a meal, here are some of the statements that you need to understand.

¡A poner la mesa! (Set the table!)

Aquí están los platos y los vasos. (Here are the dishes and glasses.)

¿Qué cubiertos? (What cutlery?)

Cuchara, cuchillo, tenedor, y cucharita. (Spoon, knife, fork, and coffee or demitasse spoon.)

Aquí están las servilletas. (Here are the napkins.)

Más sal en el salero. (More salt in the salt shaker.)

During situations involving giving or receiving foods and beverages, here are some phrases you will most probably be told or may speak yourself:

¡Buen provecho! (Enjoy your meal! — the equivalent of the French Bon appetit!)

¿Con qué está servido? (What does it come with?)

Está caliente. (It's hot [temperature].)

Está frío. (It's cold.)

Está picante. (It's hot [flavor/spice].)

Es sabroso. (It's tasty.)

Lamento, no tenemos . . . (Sorry, we don't have . . .)

¿Qué ingredientes tiene? (What are the ingredients?)

¿Qué más trae el plato? (What else is in the dish?)

These are your go-to words whenever you are ordering something to drink:

Escoger un vino. (Choose a wine.)

¡Salud! (Cheers!)

Tomar un refresco. (Drink a soda pop.)

Tomar un trago. (Have a drink [alcoholic].)

Un vaso de agua. (A glass of water.)

Un vaso de leche. (A glass of milk.)

THREE VERBS YOU SHOULD KNOW WHEN EATING OR DRINKING!

In Spanish, there are two verbs for drinking. One is tomar (toh-mahr); the other is beber (bveh-bvehr).

TAKE AND DRINK WITH TOMAR

Tomar literally means and often means exactly that, but when talking about drinking a soda, tomar un refresco, not literally drinking one and tomar is usually followed by what kind of drinking you are drinking.

Tomar is a regular verb of the -ar (ahr) group. The root of the verb is tom- (tohm), as you can see from the table that follows:

Conjugation

yo tomo

tú tomas

él, ella, ello, uno, usted toma

nosotros tomamos

vosotros tomáis

ellos, ellas, ustedes toman

DRINKING UP WITH BEBER

With beber, you are sure that this verb is only applied to drinking.

Beber (bveh-bvehr) is also a regular verb; it's from the -er (ehr) group. The root of the verb is: beb- (bvehbv), as you can see in the following table:

Conjugation

yo bebo

tú bebes

él, ella, ello, uno, usted bebe

nosotros bebemos

vosotros bebéis

ellos, ellas, ustedes beben

MUNCHING UP WITH COMER

Comer literally means to eat. A regular verb from the -er (ehr) group, the root of this verb is com (kohm), as the following table shows:

Conjugation

yo como

tú comes

él, ella, ello, uno, usted come

nosotros comemos

vosotros coméis

ellos, ellas, ustedes comen

TRYING THE EXOTIC CUISINE

When a menu is written in a foreign language, it can be overwhelming to be approached. However, what is a little try when you know you would be trying out tasty and exotic foods! You do not want to miss them, so be familiar with the following:

- Agua, though in Mexico, meaning water which is also its exact translation, can also mean a drink made with sugar, fruit, and water. All fruits and vegetables make really refreshing aguas.
- In Chile, aguita (little water) can be an herb tea served after a meal.
- Empanada means exactly bread. However, in Mexico, an empanada is often characterized by folded and stuffed corn tortillas. You can have empanadas made out of wheat dough, always folded and stuffed, in Argentine and Chile. Argentinians like their empanadas small while it is the other way around for Chiles. Whichever way, empanadas are really delicious!
- A tortilla in Spain is a potato, onion, and egg omelette that is often served at room temperature.
- In Mexico, eloteis the name of tender corn, the kind you eat from the cob. The same thing in Argentina, Chile, Peru, and Bolivia is called choclo.
- Ejotes is a term for green beans in Mexico. Porotos verdes or porotitos is their terms when you find yourself in South America. In most of Spanish-speaking America, when beans are dry, they are called porotos. In Mexico they are known as frijoles. In a Peruvian market, there is a great variety of beans. They come in different colors, shapes, and sizes that will sure make your mouth water. You should try them all.
- The cut of beef called sirloin in the United States is termed filete in Chile. In Argentine, lomo is the term for the same cut of beef.

- Bife con papas y ensalada, which means grilled steak with potatoes and salad is the basic Argentinian meal. On a setting of an Argentinean grill, you are likely to find a number of meats that are familiar to you along with other that you probably never have eaten. Chinchulín, which is braided and grilled beef bowels, are among the exotic delicacies. Molleja, which is the thyroid gland of a cor is another delicacy. Delicioso!
- In Mexico, molleja is the term for chicken gizzard. In Chile, the same chicken gizzard is called contre.
- Pana refers to the liver that you eat in Chile while in most places of Latin America, the liver is called hígado.
- In Spain, jamón serrano, salt cured ham typical of the mountain regions, is a great delicacy.
- If you love fish and seafood, the places to go are Chile and Peru. The best fish in the world swim in the Humboldt Current, coming from Antarctica.
- You find delights such as loco, a truly gigantic scallop, and congrio, or conger eel, a type of fish.
- You can also find albacora (swordfish), cangrejo (giant crab), jaiba (small crab), langosta (lobster); langostino (prawn), camarón (shrimp), and other delights to crowd your sopa marinera (fish soup).
- In Peru, they make ceviche out of raw fish or raw seafood. Ceviches come in many varieties. One commonality is that Latinos like their ceviche very hot. In ceviche, raw fish or seafood is marinated in lemon juice, salt, and hot peppers. The fish or seafood is still raw after this treatment, but it looks less transparent, as though it were cooked. Sensational!
- You also may want to order some of these specialties:
- Called aguacate in Mexico and palta in Argentina, Uruguay, and Chile, it's still the same avocado.
- In the south of Mexico, when you say pan meaning bread, people usually think of something that the baker made to taste sweet. In South America, pan is closer to what you eat in the States.

- Torta in Mexico is a sandwich in a bun but most everywhere else in Latin America, torta means cake, and sandwich means sandwich no matter how it's served.
- Memelas in Mexico are tortillas that are pinched on the side to form a hollow, which is filled with pastes and delicacies.
- Gazpacho, is a chilled vegetable soup from Spain flavored with olive oil, garlic, and vinegar.
- In Spain, paella is a favorite dish made of seafood and saffron rice.

How do you like your salsa?

Some people say that what's truly special about Latin American foods is the sauce. This statement is especially true of the sauces served in Mexico, which have an infinite variety of flavors and textures.

MOLE: TRULY HOT SAUCES

- Mole is a word used that means sauce in Mexico. They are often served hot with meats and chicken:
- Mole negro (black mole) looks black — naturally! — and is made with all toasted ingredients: cocoa, chilies, almonds, onions, garlic, and bread. It can be very spicy or less so.
- Mole colorado (red mole) looks red and is made with chilies. It's spicy hot! The sauce is also called coloradito.
- Mole amarillo (yellow mole) is orangy yellow. You make it with almonds and raisins, among other ingredients. Generally, it's only mildly spicy.
- Mole verde (green mole) is made with green tomatoes, green chilies (hot peppers), and coriander (cilantro) and looks green. It can be very spicy or mildly hot.
- Mexicans don't eat moles every day. These delicacies are served only on special occasions. Tourists are luckier — they can find them all the time.

CHILLED HOT SAUCES

To add more spices in their food, Mexicans bring some cold sauces.

- Pico de gallo, which translates as rooster's beak is made totally with vegetables. It looks red, green, and white because it's made with tomatoes, jalapeño peppers, coriander, and onions. Hot!
- Guacamole needs no translation. It's the dip made with avocado, chili "hot pepper," coriander (cilantro), lemon, and salt. It's sometimes spicy hot.
- Salsa verde green sauce is made with green tomatoes, chilies, and coriander. Hot!
- Salsa roja red sauce is made with red tomatoes and chilies. Hot!

MAKING A RESTAURANT RESERVATION

The following dialogue shows how a restaurant reservation is usually made.

Note, however, that a vast majority of restaurants in Latin America do not necessarily need reservations.

Señor Jesal wants to take his wife to a nice restaurant on her birthday. Listen in as he calls the restaurant to make reservations.

> Señor Jesal: Quiero reservar una mesa para dos personas. (I want to reserve a table for two people.)
>
> Waiter: ¡Cómo no! ¿Para qué hora será? (Of course! At what time?)
>
> Señor: Para las ocho de la noche. (At eight o'clock in the evening.)
>
> Waiter: ¿A nombre de quién? (Under what name?)
>
> Señor: El señor Jesal. (Mr. Jesal)
>
> Waiter: Bien, les esperamos. (Good, we'll look forward to seeing you.)

Señor Jesal:Muchas gracias. (Many thanks.)

ORDERING UP SOME FOOD WITH THE VERB QUERER

To convey a want or a wish, use the verb "querer."

Querer is an irregular verb. Notice that the root quer- is transformed into quier- with most subject pronouns.

Conjugation	Pronunciation
yo quiero	yoh keeeh-roh
tú quieres	too keeeh-rehs
él, ella, ello, uno, usted quiere	ehl, eh-yah, eh-yoh, oo-noh, oos-tehd keeeh-reh
nosotros queremos	noh-soh-trohs keh-reh-mohs
vosotros queréis	bvoh-soh-trohs keh-rehees
ellos, ellas, ustedes quieren	eh-yohs, eh-yahs, oos-teh-dehs keeeh-rehn

The following dialogue shows you querer in action.

Calling a waiter

A waiter in Argentina is a mozo (moh-soh) or a young man. However, it is offensive in Chile to call somebody mozo. In Chile, they derived their term for a young man from a French word similary pronounced and spelled as garcon. Thus, they say it as garzón when referring to a young man.

It is better to call the waiter joven, which means young and even if he is not that young anymore in order to get his attention. Calling the waiter by the terms above will only cause him no reaction.

Moreover, in Spain, a waiter is a camarero

When a woman is serving you, call her simply señorita. This means Miss, no matter where you are.

ORDERING A BEVERAGE

If you want to order a beverage to drink with your food, you may participate in a conversation similar to this one.

> Waiter: ¿Quieren algo para beber? (Do you want anything to drink?)
>
> ¿Se sirven un agua de frutas? (Would you like a diluted fruit juice?)
>
> Señora Rica: No, yo quiero un vaso de vino tinto. (No, I want a glass of red wine.)
>
> Waiter: Muy bien, ¿y usted? (Very well, and you?)
>
> Señor Jesal: Yo quiero una cerveza. (I want a beer.)
>
> Waiter: ¿Lager o negra? (Lager or dark?)
>
> Señor Jesal: Prefiero negra. (I prefer dark.)

MAKING A RESTAURANT ORDER

The following conversation is a typical setting for a restaurant order exchange.

Now for great eating! You can use the following conversation as an example to order some soup or salad.

> Waiter: ¿Están listos para ordenar? (Are you ready to order?)
> Señora Rica: Yo quiero una ensalada mixta. (I want a mixed [several vegetables] salad.)
> Señor Jesal: Y para mí una sopa de mariscos. (And for me, seafood soup.)
> Waiter: ¿Y de plato fuerte? (And as the main course?)

Señor Jesal: ¿Qué nos recomienda? (What do you suggest?)

Waiter: Tenemos dos platos especiales: mole amarillo con carne de res y huachinango a la veracruzana. (We have two specials: yellow mole with beef and red snapper Veracruz style.)

Señora Rica: ¿Qué es el huachinango a la veracruzana? (What is red snapper Veracruz style?)

Waiter: Es pescado con tomates, chile, cilantro, y cebolla. (It's fish with tomatoes, hot peppers, coriander (cilantro), and onions.)

Señora Rica: Yo quiero pollo frito. (I want fried chicken.)

Waiter: No tenemos pollo frito. Tenemos pollo asado en salsa de mango. (We don't have fried chicken. We have broiled chicken with mango sauce.)

Señora Rica: ¿Con qué está acompañado? (What does it come with?)

Waiter: Con elotes frescos, y calabazas entomatadas. (With fresh corn, and zucchini in tomato sauce.)

Señora Rica: Bueno, voy a probar el pollo con mango. (Good, I'll try the chicken with mango.)

PAYING THE BILL

Whenever settling the bill, one usually states it with la cuenta, which means to check. The upcoming conversation shows the same scenario and also leaving a tip.

You will most probably say a thing like this when you pay the bill.

Señor Jesal: Joven, ¿nos trae la cuenta por favor? (Waiter, will you bring us the check please?)

Waiter: Ya vuelvo con la cuenta. (I'll be back with the check.)

Señor Jesal: ¿Aceptan tarjetas de crédito? (Do you accept credit cards?)

Waiter: No, lo lamento mucho, aquí no aceptamos tarjetas de crédito. (No, I'm very sorry; we don't take credit cards.)

A bit later:

> Señora Rica: ¿Ya pagamos la cuenta? (We paid the check already?)
>
> Señor Jesal: Ya la pagué. (I paid it already.)
>
> Señora Rica: ¿Dejamos propina? (Did we leave a tip?)
>
> Señor Jesal: Sí dejé propina. Yes, I left a tip.

TAKING A BATHROOM BREAK

Whenever going out, you will have to wash your hands, freshen your make-up, or do something else that requires using the powder room. Like in States and Canada, bathrooms in Latin America show elegance as the exclusivity of the restaurant becomes more apparent. The more expensive the restaurant is, the more elegant the bathroom will be. The following phrases will help you find the room you need.

> ¿Dónde están los baños? (Where are the bathrooms?)
> Los baños están al fondo, a la derecha. (The bathrooms are at the back, to the right.)
> ¿Es este el baño? (Is this the bathroom?)
> No, este no es el baño. Es ese. (No, this isn't the bathroom. It's that one.)

Here are more food-related one-liners:

> ¿Puede recomendar un bar? (Can you recommend a bar?)
> ¿Puede recomendar un café? (Can you recommend a cafe?)
> ¿Puede recomendar un restaurante? (Can you recommend a restaurant?)
> ¿Siguen sirviendo comida? (Are you still serving food?)
> ¿Cuánto hay que esperar? (How long is the wait?)
> ¿Adónde se va para ...? (Where would you go for (a) ...?)
> celebrar (celebration)
> comer barato (cheap meal)
> comer comida típica (local specialities)
> Quisiera reservar una mesa para ... (I'd like to reserve a table for ...)

(dos) personas ((two) people)

las (ocho) ((eight) o'clock)

Lo siento, hemos cerrado. (Sorry, we're closed.)

No tenemos mesa. (We have no tables.)

Un momento. (One moment.)

Quisiera una mesa para (dos), por favor. (I'd like a table for (two), please.)

Quisiera la lista de bebidas, por favor. (I'd like the drink list, please.)

Quisiera el menú, por favor. (I'd like the menu, please.)

¿Tienen ... ? (Do you have ...?)

comidas para niños (children's meals)

un menú en inglés (a menu in English)

AT THE RESTAURANT

¿Es de autoservicio? (Is it self-serve?)

¿La cuenta incluye servicio? (Is service included in the bill?)

¿Qué recomienda? (What would you recommend?)

Tomaré lo mismo que ellos. (I'll have what they're having.)

¿Tarda mucho en prepararse? (Does it take long to prepare?)

¿Que lleva ese plato? (What's in that dish?)

¿Éstos son gratis? (Are these complimentary?)

Sólo queremos tomar algo. (We're just having drinks.)

Quisiera un plato típico. (I'd like a local speciality.)

Reservado (Reserved)

Por favor nos trae ... (Please bring ...)

oon va·so (a glass)

una servilleta (a servietteo

una copa de vino (a wineglass)

Do you like ...? (listen for ...)

le goos·ta ... (¿Le gusta ...?)

Recomiendo ... (I suggest the ...)

How would you like that cooked? (¿Cómo lo quiere preparado?)

APERITIVOS (APPETISERS)

Caldos (Soups)

Cervezas (Beers)

De Entrada (Entrees)

Digestivos (Digestifs)

Ensaladas (Salads)

Licores (Spirits)

Desserts (Postres)

Refrescos (Soft Drinks)

SEGUNDOS PLATOS (MAIN COURSES)

Vinos Blancos (White Wines)

Vinos Dulces (Dessert Wines)

Vinos Espumosos (Sparkling Wines)

Vinos Tintos (Red Wines)

HABLANDO DE COMIDA (TALKING FOOD)

Me encanta este plato. (I love this dish.)

Nos encanta la comida típica de la zona. (We love the local cuisine.)

¡Estaba buenísimo! (That was delicious!)

Mi enhorabuena al cocinero. (My compliments to the chef.)

Estoy lleno/a. m/f (I'm full.)

Esto está ... (This is ...)

quemado (burnt)

(too) cold ((muy) frío)

exquisito (superb)

LAS COMIDAS (BREAKFAST)

¿Cómo es un típico (desayuno) español? (What's a typical Spanish (breakfast)?)

Tortilla (omelette)

Muesli (muesli)

Toast (tostadas)

LA BEBIDA (DRINK)

LAS BEBIDAS NO ALCOHÓLICAS (NON-ALCOHOLIC DRINKS)

No bebo alcohol. (I don't drink alcohol.)

Quisiera un café. (I'd like a cup of coffee.)

Quisiera un té. (I'd like a cup of tea.)

con leche (with milk)

sin azúcar (without sugar)

refrescos (soft drink)

zumo (de naranja) ((orange) juice)

agua hervida (boiled water)

agua mineral (mineral water)

con gas (sparkling)

LAS BEBIDAS ALCOHÓLICAS (ALCOHOLIC DRINKS)

cerveza (f) (beer)

coñac (brandy)

champán (champagne)

combinado (cocktail)

sangria (red-wine punch)

un chupito m de (güisqui) (a shot of (whisky)

gin (ginebra)

ron (rum)

tequila (tequila)

vodka (vodka)

A BIG FAN OF THE MINI

A lot of Spanish bars provide massive plastic beakers of beer to cater to young revellers. It's cut with water and average tasting – but cheap and free flowing! These fountains of froth are called minis.

Here are some helpful phrases if you are going to order a brew:

cerveza f... (... beer)

de barril (draught)

negra (dark)

rubia (light)

sin alcohol (nonalcoholic)

botellín (small bottle of beer (250 ml))

jarra (jug)

litrona (litre bottle of beer)

mediana (bottle of beer (300 ml))

pinta (pint)

una botella de vino tinto (a bottle of red wine)

una copa de vino tinto (a glass of red wine)

una botella de vino blanco (a bottle of white wine)

una copa de vino blanco (a glass of white wine)

vino ... (... wine)

dulce (dessert)

rosado (rose)

espumoso (sparkling)

una botella de cerveza (a bottle of beer)

una caña de cerveza (a glass of beer)

¿UNA DE MÁS? (ONE TOO MANY?)

salud (cheers)

Lo siento, pero no me apetece. (Thanks, but I don't feel like it.)

Me lo estoy pasando muy bien. (This is hitting the spot.)

Estoy cansado/a, mejor me voy a casa. m/f (I'm tired, I'd better go home.)

¿Dónde está el lavabo? (Where's the toilet?)

Esto me está subiendo mucho. (I'm feeling drunk.)

¡Me siento fenomenal! (I feel fantastic!)

SPANISH CELEBRATIONS

Shaped in the pre-Columbian times and myths brought from Africa, Spain has formed holidays and feasts that always call for celebration. Christian myths and religion have brought new and peculiar celebrations that have shaped the face of holidays. The list includes the following:

Año Nuevo: In other culture, this is most commonly called the New Year's Eve Party. However, in the bubble of Spain, people celebrate the Fiesta de Año Nuevo. During the night of December 31, wherever you go there will be party-goers and revellers just moving around. Moreover, this continues until the morning of January 1. These party-goers often cheer for the New Year in Spanish. They usually sing and shout **¡Salud!, ¡Feliz Año Nuevo!** which means *Cheers, Happy New Year!*

La Fiesta de Reyes: This is the most awaited holiday by children in Spain and most of Latin America. Dated on January 6, La Fiesta de Reyes is a celebration for giving presents to the children. It is called "Three Kings" in places outside of Latin America. In Spain, moreover, this is famously called **la epifanía** which celebrates the visit of the Three Kings to Bethlehem. Because the Kings brought present to the baby Jesus, children have a role in this holiday which is getting their own presents. During this holiday, all business and normal endeavors stop and families do spend the day with their children. It is nice to be a child in this Reyes. However, adults do not get gifts.

Paradura del Niño: Since Spain is a center for religion, they also have the longest festivity for the birth of Jesus. It starts at Christmas and continues until the beginning of February. In Venezuela, specifically the Andean Region, people have their own way of enjoying the time of celebrating *The Hosting, Stealing, and Searching for the Child* or **La Paradura, Robo, y Búsqueda del Niño.** The figure of Jesus as a child is "stolen" from the manger representation in somebody's house, which instigates a search. The person who does the act of stealing the Child is a neighbour, and the ploy is like hide-and-seek. Thus, the Child is hidden somewhere. Whoever will find the Child will host the party on the second of February which is called the **Fiesta de la Candelaria** and **Fiesta de la Purificación.**

Carnaval: In the Spanish-speaking world, like Bolivia, Oruro, Cartagena, Colombia, Veracruz, Mexico, Ciudad Real, and Santa Cruz de Tenerife, Carnaval or most famously known Mardi Gras before the arrival of Lent. Mardi Gras is a feast of dancing, singing, and excess before the time of moderation and fasting.

Viernes Santo: Most commonly known as Good Friday, this day, many Spanish-speaking countries display exceptional ceremonies and events. This is a remembrance of the crucifixion of Jesus and is incorporated by real enactments of the event. The Biblical story is re-enacted in one large play participated by whole communities. For the role of Jesus, one person is crucified while the other village actors recite the New Testament texts.

Día de la Madre: In English term, this is Mother's Day. This is celebrated anywhere just like the way it is celebrated in Mexico on May 10. Even across the world, people travel to come home because they put this day on a pedestal. Who wouldn't be when it is their mothers' day? For Mexicans, this day will be shown abundantly. Mothers are celebrated, toasted and showered with presents. Even people outside the family joins the celebration by greeting every woman who is also a mother that they come across the street. Families gather on this day like how families in the United States and Canada gather for Christmas.

Día de los Muertos: On November 2, people celebrate El Día de los Muertos which is their way of honouring their dead relatives. People in Andean countries and Mexico believe that on this day, the departed visits their home. They welcome these people with offers of the things the one who left used to love. They would often prepare flowers, favourite candies and even favourite food of the departed. This remembering of the dead is a celebration of the harvests and of plenty.

VIAJAR (TRAVEL)
GRASPING SPATIAL DIRECTIONS
When going somewhere, it is essential that you completely understand directions, especially when you are being used as the reference or something else. Here are some terms to describe relationships:

   al lado (beside, next to, at the side of)

   al frente (in front of)

   dentro (inside)

   adentro (inside; because dentro also means inside, adentro may express movement, as when someone or something moves toward an interior)

   fuera (outside)

   afuera (outside; can express movement, as in the case of adentro — the fourth bullet point in this list)

   bajo (under; below)

debajo (underneath)

arriba (ah-ree-bvah) (above)

Practicing these directions comes in handy. The sentences that follow use spatial-direction terms:

La pastelería está al lado del banco. (The pastry shop is next to the bank.)

Al frente del banco hay una zapatería. (In front of the bank there is a shoe store.)

Las mesas del café están afuera. (The tables of the cafe are outside.)

Cuando llueve ponen las mesas adentro. (When it rains they put the tables inside.)

Arriba hay cielo despejado. (Above, the sky is clear.)

Hay agua bajo los pies de Carlos. (There's water under Carlos's feet.)

Debajo de la calle corre el tren subterráneo. (The subway runs under the street.)

Este ascensor va arriba. (This elevator goes up.)

Hay un gato dentro de la caja. (There's a cat inside the box.)

ESENCIALES (SAFE TRAVEL ESSENTIALS)

In travelling, although some things are already planned, you still come across a spur of spontaneous events. It is always better to know how to ask help when the unexpected happens.

¡Socorro! (Help!)

¡Pare! (Stop!)

¡Váyase! (Go away!)

¡Ladrón! (Thief!)

¡Fuego! (Fire!)

¡Cuidado! (Watch out!)

Es una emergencia. (It's an emergency.)

¡Llame a la policía! (Call the police!)

¡Llame a un médico! (Call a doctor!)

¡Llame a una ambulancia! (Call an ambulance!)

Estoy enfermo/a. (I'm ill.)

Mi amigo/a está enfermo/a. (My friend is ill.)

¿Me puede ayudar, por favor? (Could you help me, please?)

Necesito usar el teléfono. (I have to use the telephone.)

Estoy perdido/a. (I'm lost.)

¿Dónde están los servicios? (Where are the toilets?)

¡Déjame en paz! (Leave me alone!)

LA POLICIA (THE POLICE)

While we ado not wishfor anything unfortunate to happen, it is always better to know where to run, what to say and how to say it in times of emergency. Here are some phrases that can guide you:

¿Dónde está la comisaría? (Where's the police station?)

Quiero denunciar un delito. (I want to report an offence.)

Tengo seguro. (I have insurance.)

Él/Ella intentó asaltarme. (He/She tried to assault me.)

Él/Ella intentó robarme. (He/She tried to rob me.)

Me han robado. (I've been robbed.)

He sido violado/a. (I've been raped.)

He perdido mis maletas. (I've lost my bags.)

He perdido mi dinero. (I've lost my money.)

He perdido mi pasaporte. (I've lost my passport.)

Lo siento. (I apologise.)

No sabía que estaba haciendo algo mal. (I didn't realise I was doing anything wrong.)

Soy inocente. (I'm innocent.)

Quiero ponerme en contacto con mi consulado (I want to contact my consulate.)

Quiero ponerme en contacto con mi embajada. (I want to contact my embassy.)

¿Puedo llamar a un abogado? (Can I call a lawyer?)

Necesito un abogado que hable inglés. (I need a lawyer who speaks English.)

¿Podemos pagar una multa al contado? (Can I pay an on-the-spot fine?)

Esta droga es para uso personal. (This drug is for personal use.)

Tengo receta para esta droga. (I have a prescription for this drug.)

¿De qué me acusan? (What am I accused of?)

There is a possibility for the police to say:

El plazo de tu visado se ha pasado. (You have overstayed your visa.)

Será acusado/a de ... m/f (You'll be charged with ...)

Él/Ella será acusado/a de ... (He'll/She'll be charged with ...)

asalto (assault)

posesión (de sustancias ilegales) (possession (of illegal substances))

ratería (shoplifting)

exceso de velocidad (speeding)

REFERRING TO A MAP

When all else fails, you should be able to know how to refer to a map. The following terminologies will help you know directions that will deliver you to the right place:

el norte (the north)

el sur (the south)

el este (the east)

el oriente (the east [Literally: where the sun originates])

el oeste (the west)

el poniente (the west [Literally: where the sun sets])

Maps are basically your guide to getting around a foreign place. The first thing that you should do upon arriving is buying a map or requesting the car rental office to provide you with a map. You can get around with more ease if you know how to interpret a map or if there is a local guide to do it for you. Here are some mapping phrases that you can absolutely check out:

La avenida Venus está al este de aquí. (Venus Avenue is east of here.)

Al oeste se encuentra la calle Las Violetas. (To the west is Violetas Street.)

El parque está al norte. (The park is to the north.)

Al sur se va hacia el río. (To the south is the river. [Literally: To the south, one goes toward the river.])

El oriente es donde el sol se levanta. (The east is where the sun rises.)

El poniente es donde el sol se pone. (The west is where the sun sets.)

Jordania está en el Cercano Oriente. (Jordan is in the Near East.)

China está en el Lejano Oriente. (China is in the Far East.)

América está al oriente del Océano Pacífico. (America is east of the Pacific Ocean.)

Asia está al poniente del océano. (Asia is west of the ocean.)

The following phrases are helpful when asking or giving general directions:

la calle (the street)

la avenida (the avenue)

el bulevar (the boulevard)

el río (the river)

la plaza (the square)

el parque (the park)

el jardín (the garden; sometimes a small park)

el barrio (the neighborhood)

la cuadra (the block)

la manzana (the block)

izquierda (left)

derecha (right)

derecho (straight)

doblar (to turn)

seguir (to follow)

Asking for directions can be confusing. For locals, they usually forget the idea that you are foreign to the city and the answer is not that obvious to you – however the best way to deal with this is to listen intently and understand the concept of what they are saying. More so, here are some phrases you should start practicing.

En el barrio hay una avenida ancha. (In the neighborhood, there is a wide avenue.)

Nuestra calle va de norte a sur. (Our street runs north to south.)

Mi tía vive en la Cerrada del Olivo. (My aunt lives at the Cerrada [street with no exit] del Olivo [olive tree].)

Junto al río hay un gran parque. (On the riverside there is a large park.)

La plaza está en el centro de la ciudad. (The square is in the center of the city.)

En el jardín hay juegos para niños. (In the small park, they have a children's playground.)

El Zócalo de México es una plaza enorme. (The Zocalo in Mexico is an immense square.)

Esa avenida se llama La Alameda. (The name of that avenue is La Alameda.)

The situation below is an example of how to ask directions when touring the city:

Ella is an artist who's anxious to visit the Graphics Museum. She plans to walk there from her hotel so she can avoid the heavy traffic.

Ella: Disculpe, ¿cómo llego al Museo de la Estampa? (Excuse me, how do I get to the Graphics Museum?)

Receptionist: Muy fácil. Está muy cerca. (Very easy. It's very close.)

Sale del hotel. (You go out of the hotel.)

Ella: ¿Dónde está la salida? (Where is the exit?)

Receptionist: La salida está a la derecha. (The exit is to the right.)

Al salir va hacia la izquierda (As you get out, you go to the left)

camina hasta la segunda calle (walk to the second street)

da vuelta a la derecha, una cuadra (turn to the right, go one block)

y llega al museo. (and you arrive at the museum.)

Ella: Gracias por su ayuda. (Thanks for your help.)

HERE, THERE AND EVERYWHERE

Here and there is indicated in two ways for the Spanish people. Native Spanish speakers interchange here and there often, with no distinction between the two words. Here and there are adverbs; they always work in the vicinity of a verb and words that talk about space:

allá (there)

allí (there)

acá (here)

aquí (here)

Here are some sentences showing the use of the words above:

Allí, en la esquina, está el banco. (There, on the corner, is the bank.)

Allá van los turistas. (There go the tourists.)

Aquí se come muy bien. (Here one eats very well.)

Acá está el museo. (Here is the museum.)

¡Ven acá! (Come here!)

¡Corre allá! (Run there!)

MORE TRAVEL-RELATED WORDS!

viajar – to travel

el mundo – world

la región – region

el kilómetro – kilometer

los Estados Unidos – United States

la cultura – culture

la lengua – language

el español – Spanish language

el castellano – Spanish language

la nación – nation

la libertad – liberty, freedom

el norte – north

el oeste – west

el sur – south

el este – east

explorar – to explore

el presidente – president

la situación – situation

el líder – leader

la reunión – meeting

el país – country

la capital – capital city

la inmigración – immigration

legal – legal

ilegal – illegal

traducir – to translate

visitar – to visit

el intercambio – exchange

EL TRANSPORTE / TRANSPORTATION

In Spain, there are different means of transportation. Some go by cab. Some go by train. Others like to immerse in the city by walking. Whichever your preference is, here are some transportation-related statements that you can refer to.

Van a la capital en tren. (They're going to the capital by train.)

¿Se puede ir en transporte público? (Can we get there by public transport?)

¿Se puede ir en bici? (Can we get there by bike?)

Prefiero ir a pie. (I'd prefer to walk there.)

MORE TRANSPORT WORDS!

a pie – by foot

caminar – to walk

andar – to walk, to go

la bicicleta – bicycle

montar – to ride

montar en bicicleta – to ride

a bicycle el carro – car

el coche – car el

automóvil – car

conducir – to drive

manejar – to drive

el taxi – taxi

el autobús – bus

el metro – subway

el tren – train

el barco – boat

el avión – airplane

volar (o à ue) – to fly

EL AVIÓN (TAKING THE PLANE)

¿Cuándo sale el próximo vuelo para ...? (When's the next flight to ...?)

¿A qué hora tengo que facturar mi equipaje? (What time do I have to check in?)

EL AUTOBÚS (BUS)

¿Qué autobús/autocar va a ...? (Which city/intercity bus goes to ...?)

Éste/Ése. (This/That one.)

El autobús número ... (Bus number ...)

¿Puede avisarme cuando lleguemos a ...? (Please tell me when we get to ...)

EL TREN (TRAIN)

¿Cuál es esta estación? (What station is this?)

¿Cuál es la próxima estación? (What's the next station?)

¿Para el tren en (Madrid)? (Does this train stop at (Madrid)?)

¿Tengo que cambiar de tren? (Do I need to change trains?)

¿Cuál es el coche ...? (Which carriage is ...?)

de primera clase (1st class)

para (Madrid) (for (Madrid))

comedor (for dining)

EL BARCO (BOAT)

¿Hay chalecos salvavidas? (Are there life jackets?)

¿Cómo está el mar hoy? (What's the sea like today?)

Estoy mareado. (I feel seasick.)

EL TAXI (TAXI)

Quisiera un taxi. (I'd like a taxi.)

Quisiera un taxi a (las nueve de la mañana). (I'd like a taxi at (9am).)

Quisiera un taxi mañana. (I'd like a taxi tomorrow.)

¿Está libre este taxi? (Is this taxi available?)

¿Cuánto cuesta ir a ...? (How much is it to ...?)

Por favor, ponga el taxímetro. (Please put the meter on.)

Por favor, lléveme a (esta dirección). (Please take me to (this address).)

Voy con mucho retraso. (I'm really late.)

¿Cuánto es en total? (How much is the final fare?)

Por favor vaya más despacio. (Please slow down.)

Por favor espere aquí. (Please wait here.)

Por favor pare aquí. (Please stop here.)

SHOPPING

Shopping savvies can still find themselves enjoying at new stores to shop at and imploring new ways to shop. Imagine having to shop beyond the borders of the United States. It is very entertaining plus you can find great deals. However, whether shopping is an easy-peasy or something that stresses you out, you will find that in this chapter you will be taught how to shop the Latin way!

Going in a foreign place will not be complete if you do not check out their open-air market or small boutiques. This is one way of knowing a country. In larger cities across the world, people really do check out department stores as much as they do in the United States. When you are in a foreign land, try to schedule a shopping trip to a major department store. This is one way to witness how and where locals get their clothes and other necessities. In department stores, you will also find prices that are clearly posted and labeled. Moreover, you will find items that have local touches in it. However, if you are the one who wants to find exotic items sold in an old-fashioned way, a department store is not the ideal place for you. Exotic clothes and objects are sold in markets where the shopping experience will surely of a different vibe.

In this chapter, you will find out how to make the most of your shopping experience by knowing what exactly to say in shopping scenarios.

For some pointers, not every country has that of the shopping situation in Canada or the States. Often times, there are merchandises that do not have all the information you need. There is a need to communicate with the salesperson still. However, this information can be a little bit fuzzy. In situations like this, you have to trust your senses as well as your experience.

¿Dónde está la entrada? (Where's the entrance?)

¿Dónde está la salida? (Where's the exit?)

empuje (push)

tire (pull)

jale (pull [in Mexico])

el ascensor (the elevator)

la escalera mecánica (the escalator)

el vendedor or la vendedora (the salesperson [male and female])

la caja (the check out stand)

If you are planning your day and you want to know about the store hours, you may try the following statements:

¿A qué hora abren? (At what time do you [formal] open?)

¿A qué hora cierran? (At what time do you [formal] close?)

It is already in Spain's shopping culture that salespeople love to be as involved as they can in the customer's shopping experience. They like to make their customers feel like a royalty or be pampered. However, if you only want to browse, just be firm on how you want to have your shopping experience. Here's how to tell a salesperson that you want just to browse around the store.

Salesperson: ¿Busca algo en especial? (Looking for something special?)

Olivia: Quiero mirar, no más. (I just want to look.)

Salesperson: Me llama cuando me necesita. (Call me when you need me.)

Olivia: Sí, le voy a llamar, gracias. (Yes, I'll call you, thank you.)

PROBAR (TO TRY)

The verb probar means to try and may be used quite a lot when you are shopping. Now that you know what probar is, you may ask to try on anything before you buy it. People have varied body types, and not all have a body like that of the regulars in Latin.

The dialogue below will show how to find the department store that you need.

Olivia: ¿Dónde están los vestidos de señora? (Where are the ladies' clothes?)

Salesperson: En el quinto piso. (On the fifth floor.)

Olivia: ¿Dónde está la ropa de hombre? (Where are the men's clothes?)

43

Salesperson: En el cuarto piso. (On the fourth floor.)

Olivia: ¿Dónde encuentro artículos de tocador? (Where do I find toiletries?)

Salesperson: Al fondo, a la izquierda. (At the back, to the left.)

Olivia: Busco la sección de ropa blanca. (I'm looking for sheets and towels.)

Salesperson: Un piso más arriba. (One floor up.)

Olivia: ¿Venden electrodomésticos? (Do you sell appliances?)

Salesperson: Sí, en el último piso. (Yes, on the top floor.

The next dialogue shows an approach on how to ask a salesperson for help.

Olivia accidentally split her skirt bending down to pick up some boxes at work. She needs a new one quick — one with pockets to hold the art supplies she needs as a graphic designer. She asks a salesperson for help:

Olivia: ¿Me ayuda por favor? (Will you help me, please?)

Busco una falda con bolsillos. (I'm looking for a skirt with pockets.)

Salesperson: ¿Qué talla tiene? (What's your size?)

Olivia: Talla doce americana. (Size twelve, American.)

Salesperson: ¿Me permite medirla, para estar seguras? (May I take your measurements to be sure?)

Ah, su talla es treinta y ocho. (Ah, your size is 38.)

¿Qué color busca? (What color are you looking for?)

Olivia: Rojo. (Red.)

Salesperson: ¿La quiere con flores? (Do you want it with flowers?)

Olivia: No, lisa, por favor. (No, plain, please.)

SHOPPING FOR CLOTHES

A friendly reminder: Like in the United States and Canada, the sizes of men's shirts are the same, even in Spanish-speaking countries. However, checking the fit remains to be a good idea. It is better to be sure than sorry.

In some areas where people are smaller, sizes vary. The medium can be a small size based on what you have grown up with. Truly, the best way to find out is to try the shirt before leaving the store. The following dialogue presents a sample fitting room conversation.

Here is an example of how you may ask to try on a pair of pants:

> Claudio: ¿Puedo probarme este pantalón? (May I try on these trousers?)
>
> Salesperson: Cómo no, por aquí. (Of course, this way.)
>
> Claudio: Me queda grande. (They are too big. (Literally: It fits me large.))
>
> Salesperson: Le busco otro. (I'll find you another.)
>
> Claudio: Este aprieta aquí. (This one is tight here.)
>
> Salesperson: A ver este. (Let's see this one.)
>
> Claudio: ¿Lo tiene en verde? (Do you have it in green?)
>
> Salesperson: Este, ¿a ver? (This one, let's see?)
>
> Claudio: Queda muy bien. (It fits very well.)

FIBER AND FABRIC TALK

Whenever you are out shopping, you may notice that some regions which perform less economically produce fabrics that are made of artificial fibers. One thing to note is that the price of these fibers actually equals the natural fibers. These words will help you inquire about the fibers of which the garments are made out of:

> pura (pure)
>
> la lana (the wool)
>
> el algodón (the cotton)
>
> la fibra (the fiber)
>
> por ciento (percent; percentage)

Here are some of the questions you may raise when getting to know the fabrics:

> ¿Este pantalón es de pura lana? (Are these pants made of pure wool?)
>
> No, es de lana con nylon. (No, they are made of wool and nylon.)
>
> ¿La camisa es de puro algodón? (Is the shirt made of pure cotton?)
>
> No, es de algodón con poliéster. (No, it's made of cotton and polyester.)
>
> ¿Cuánto algodón tiene esta tela? (How much cotton is there in this fabric?)
>
> Tiene cuarenta por ciento. (It has forty percent.)
>
> Busco ropa de fibras naturales. (I'm looking for natural fiber clothes.)
>
> También tenemos. (We have them also.)

LLEVAR - TAKE THAT!

Whenever you are out shopping in a Spanish-speaking country, be sure that you know the meaning of the verb llevar.

In Spanish to wear and to take with you are the same verb — llevar.

Chec the following examples to help you keep track of this dressing and tracking verb:

Me llevo esta camisa. (I'll take this shirt.)

El vestido que llevas es bellísimo. (The dress you have on is very beautiful.)

Llevo un regalo para ti. (I'm taking a present for you.)

Los llevo a la escuela todos los días. (I take them to school every day.)

Siempre llevo un uniforme en mi trabajo. (I always wear a uniform at my job.)

La llevo. (I'll take it.)

Another way to say to wear is vestir, which means to dress and which comes from vestido (dress).

In the conversation below, a customer tries on clothing with a salesperson helping.

The skirt is the right color, so Olivia wants to try it on to be on the safe side before she makes a final decision.

Salesperson: Pase al probador, por favor. (Please go into the fitting room.)

Olivia: ¿Dónde está? (Where is it?)

Salesperson: Por aquí. (This way.)

¿Le quedó bien? (Did it fit?)

Olivia: No, está muy apretada. (No, it's very tight.)

¿Puede traer una de talla más grande? (Can you bring a larger size?)

GETTING DISCOUNT!

When a price is getting a hit on your pocket, it will not hurt to ask for some bargain. Consider the statements below:

Es muy caro. (That's too expensive.)

Puede bajar el precio? (Can you lower the price?)

Te daré ... (I'll give you ...)

MORE SHOPPING TERMS!

ayudar   (to help)

probar   (to try)

medir (to measure)

más (more)

menos (less)

liso (plain; flat)

apretado (tight)

suelto (loose)

grande (large)

pequeño (small)

la talla (the size)

el probador (the fitting room)

EL DINERO (MONEY)

Wherever you go, and whenever you go, the money will always be included in your journey. You want to go shopping, you need money. You want to go eating out, you need money. You need a cab, you need money. It is practical to say that money is what makes everything work.

When doing transactions in Spain, here are some of the statements that you have to remember.

¿Dónde hay un cajero automático? (Where's an ATM?)

¿Puedo usar mi tarjeta de crédito para sacar dinero? (Can I use my credit card to withdraw money?)

¿Cuál es el tipo de cambio? (What's the exchange rate?)

¿Cuánto hay que pagar por eso? (What's the charge for that?)

¿Cuánto cuesta esto? (How much is this?)

Cuesta demasiado. (The price is too high.)

¿Podría bajar un poco el precio? (Can you lower the price?)

Me gustaría cambiar ... (I'd like to change ...)

dinero (money)

un cheque de viajero (a travellers cheque)

¿Aceptan ...? (Do you accept ...?)

tarjetas de crédito (credit cards)

tarjetas de débito (debit cards)

cheques de viajero (travellers cheques)

¿Necesito pagar por adelantado? (Do I need to pay up front?)

¿Podría darme un recibo por favor? (Could I have a receipt please?)

Quisiera que me devuelva el dinero. (I'd like my money back.)

MORE MONEY-RELATED WORDS!

el dinero – money

el dinero en efectivo – cash

el dólar – dollar

el cajero automático – automated teller machine

el cheque – check gratis – free, at no cost

cambiar – to change, to exchange

el préstamo – loan

depositar – to deposit

retirar – to withdraw

la tarjeta de crédito – credit card

la tarjeta de débito – debit card

la transacción bancaria – bank transaction

EL TRABAJO (WORK, JOB)

One of the most common workplaces in Spain is the office. Here are some common office-related tasks:

limpiar - clean

archivar - file documents

administrar el dinero - manage money

dirigir a los demás - manage others

organizar proyectos - organize projects

manejar una computadora - operate a computer

programar computadoras - do computer programming

entrar datos - do data entry

manejar una base de datos - manage a database

usar un programa de presentación - use a presentation program

crear una hoja de cálculo - create a spreadsheet

escribir a máquina - type

manejar el procesamiento de textos - do word processing

Here is a list of common office positions:

el/la asistente/a - the assistant

el/la patrón/a - the boss

el/la cajero/a - the cashier

el/la limpiador/a - the cleaner

el/la oficinista - the clerk

el/la procesador/a de datos - the data processor

el/la conductor/a - the driver

el/la inspector/a - the inspector

el/la conserje - the janitor

el/la operador/a - the operator

el/la programador/a - programmer

el/la recepcionista - receptionist

el/la vendedor/a - salesperson

el/la secretario/a - secretary

el/la técnico/a - technician

el/la temporero/a obrero – temporary worker

Hobbies & Study Situations

HOBBIES

When it comes to the talk about hobbies, it is what you usually do, and you find time for it. It is easy to express it in English when it is your foreign language, but since you are a Spanish learner now, it is safe to say that it is also easy to express when you love doing something.

The verb "gustar" is often used to express likes and dislikes. It is usually accompanied by a direct object pronoun and sometimes by a prepositional phrase like "A mí . . ." These two aid us when you are expressing what activity you like in Spanish.

Say you want to express you liking for football. In Spanish, you say it as . . .

> *"A mí gusta el futbol."*

Here are more Spanish words for activities that you might like:

> Visitar/ir a lugares (going to places)
>
> Usar la computadora (using the computer)
>
> Tomar y editar fotos (taking and editing pictures)
>
> Leer (saying you like reading in your free time)
>
> Dibujar y pintar (saying somebody like drawing and painting)
>
> Cantar (singing)
>
> Bailar (dancing)
>
> Tocar piano/guitarra/violin (play musical instruments)
>
> Escuchar música (listen to music)
>
> Practicar deportes (play sports)
>
> Jugar videojuegos (play videogames)
>
> Ver videos peliculas (watch movies)

Here are sentences on how you express your liking for something. There is a vast arena for hobbies, and the ones listed are only among the common. Nonetheless, you can use the examples below as a template when you are talking about your hobbies.

> A ella le gusta leer libros de misterio. (She likes reading mistery books.)

Me gusta leer el periódico todos los días. (I like reading the newspaper every day)

Nos gusta tocar guitarra. (We like playing guitar)

A mí me gusta bailar ¿y a ti? (I like dancing, what about you?)

A mí me gusta mucho el dibujo. (I like drawing a lot)

Me gusta relajarme escuchando música. (I like relaxing by listening to music.)

Parece que te gusta la pintura. (It seems you like painting.)

ASKING ABOUT HOBBIES

When you are aiming for a two-way interaction about hobbies, here are some simple guides for you:

Gervy: ¿Te gusta nadar? (Do you like swimming?)

JV: Si (Yes)

Gervy: ¿Te gusta cantar baladas? (Do you like singing romantic music?)

JV: A veces (Sometimes)

Gervy: ¿A ustedes les gusta tomar fotos? (Do you like taking pictures?)

JV: A nosotros sí. (We do)

STUDIES SITUATIONS

Whenever a teacher communicates with a student, he is usually in an informal tone. He uses the tú (informal of you) whenever laying out commands and to show that the student can also communicate with him. While the teacher chooses to be informal, a student has to be formal. He uses usted, a formal form of you when speaking to a teacher to show respect for authority.

INTERACTING IN THE CLASSROOM

You have to be able to be familiar with classroom instructions as not all teachers are very fluent in English. You can get by by familiarizing these words and not get surprised or confused ofabouthat it means when you hear a teacher speaking it. Being immersed in some common commands and expressions will help you get by and maintain order and manage standard interactions:

Silencio. (Be quiet.)

¡Compórtate! (Behave!)

Trae tu libro a la clase todos los días. (Bring your book to class every day.)

Cierra tu libro. (Close your book.)

Haz las correcciones a tu tarea. (Correct your assignment.)

Vete a la oficina del director/de la directora. (Go to the principal's office.)

¡Buen trabajo! (Great job!)

Dame la tarea. (Hand me your assignment.)

Pide a tus padres a firmar este papel y devuélvemelo. (Ask your parents to sign this paper and return it to me.)

No molesta a los demás. (Don't bother others.)

Vete de la clase. (Leave the classroom.)

No se permite el chicle. (No chewing gum.)

No habla. (No talking.)

Presta atención. (Pay attention.)

Por favor siéntate. (Please be seated.)

Guárdalo, ahora mismo. (Put that away, right now.)

Habla más alto. (Speak up.)

Mañana, hay un examen sobre esta material. (Tomorrow, we are having a test on this material.)

Voltéate. (Turn around.)

Necesitas llegar a las _____ o te anotaré tarde. (You need to arrive at _____ o'clock or you'll be marked tardy.)

Necesitas entregar la tarea a tiempo. (You need to turn in your homework assignments on time.)

Siéntate y espera hasta que te toca a ti. (Have a seat and wait until it's your turn.)

Ahora puedes ponerte en la cola. (Now you can get in line.)

No cólete. (Don't cut.)

Haz una cola aquí. (Stand in line here.)

Está listo con su dinero a pagar al cajero. (Have your money ready to pay the cashier.)

No molesta a los demás mientras comen. (Don't bother others while they're eating.)

Habla con la voz baja. (Keep your voice down.)

Quédate en la mesa hasta que estás despedido. (Stay at your table until you're dismissed.)

Ahora puedes regresr a tu sala de clase. (Now you may return to your classroom.)

Ven aquí. (Come here.)

Espera tu turno. (Wait your turn.)

Llévate bien con los demás. (Play nicely.)

¡Alto! (Stop!)

No pega. (No hitting.)

Ponte a pie en un círculo. (Stand in a circle.)

Los que necesitan ir al baño, levánten las manos. (Whoever needs to go to the restroom, raise your hand.)

¿Quién necesita ir al baño? (Who needs to go to the restroom?)

Yo necesito ir al baño. (I need to go to the restroom.)

Lava las manos después de ir al baño. (Wash your hands after using the restroom.)

Quédate en la cola. (Stay in line.)

Quédate dentro de la escuela hasta que el autobús llega. (Remain inside until your bus arrives.)

Quédate en la acera. (Stay on the sidewalk.)

No empuja. (No pushing.)

No corre. (No running.)

No pisa el césped. (Stay off the grass.)

Pasa por aquí. (Step this way.)

Retrocede. (Step back.)

SCHOOL SUBJECTS

el algebra - algebra

el arte - art

la banda - band

la biología - biology

el cálculo - calculus

la química - chemistry

la informática - computer science

la geología - earth science

el inglés - English

la geografía - geography

la geometría - geometry

la salud - health

la historia - history

las artes industrials - industrial arts

las matemáticas - mathematics

la música - music

la caligrafía - penmanship

la educatión física - physical education/gym

la física - physics

la ciencia - science

los estudios sociales - social studies

el discurso - speech

la ortografía - spelling

SCHOOL SUPPLIES

un bolígrafo - ballpoint pen

un libro - book

una mochila - backpack

una calculadora - calculator

unos lápices de colores - colored pencils

unos crayones - crayons

un diccionario - dictionary

una goma de borrar - eraser

una carpeta - folder

una barra de pegamento - glue stick

unos marcadores - markers

papel - paper

con líneas - wide-ruled

sin líneas - unruled

cuadriculado - graph

una pluma - pen

un lápiz - pencil

una regla - ruler

los útiles escolares - school supplies

unas tijeras - scissors

un libro de texto - textbook

una carpeta de tres anillos - three-ring binder

Basic Vocabulary

Words change worlds. Wow the people with your knowing the Spanish vocabulary. When you hear a thing or two, you will no longer have to ask what the word means for you are already acquainted with it. That is our mission for this chapter.

Check out some basic Spanish vocabulary from A to Z.

A

a menudo: a meh-noo-doh = often

a pie: ah peeeh = walking (literally: on foot)

a rayas: ah rah-yahs = striped

a sus órdenes: a soos ohr-dehn-ehs = at your service

a veces: ah bveh-sehs = sometimes

abeja (f): ah-bveh-hah = bee

abogado/a (m, f): ah-bvoh-gah-doh/dah = lawyer

abrazarse: ah-bvrah-sahr-seh = to hug each other

abrigo (m): ah-bvree-goh = coat

abril (m): ah-bvreel = April

abrir: ah-bvreer = to open

abrocharse: ah-bvroh-chahr-seh = to fasten

absurdo: ahbv-soor-doh = absurd

abuela (f): ah-bvooeh-lah = grandmother

abuelo (m): ah-bvooeh-loh = grandfather

abuelos (m): ah-bveh-lohs = grandparents

aburrido: ah-bvoo-rree-doh = boring

aburrir: ah-bvoo-rreer = to bore

aburrirse: ah-bvoo-rreer-seh = to become bored

acabar de: ah-kah-bvahr deh = to have just

acercarse: ah-sehr-kahr-seh = to approach, to near

aconsejar: ah-kohn-seh-Hahr = to advise

acordar (ue): ah-kohr-dahr = to agree

acostar (ue): ah-kohs-tahr = to put to bed

---

acostarse (ue): ah-kohs-tahr-seh = to go to bed

actor (m): ahk-tohr = actor

actriz (f): ahk-trees = actress

actuar: ahk-tooahr = to act

adelante: ah-deh-lahn-teh = in front, ahead

adiós: ah-deeohs = good bye

aduana (f): ah-dooah-nah = customs

aeropuerto (m): ah-eh-roh-pooehr-toh = airport

afeitarse: ah-fehee-tahr-seh = to shave

afortunado: ah-fohr-too-nah-doh = fortunate

afuera: ah-fooeh-rah = outside

agencia (f): ah-Hehn-seeah = agency

agosto (m): ah-gohs-toh = August

agua (m): ah-gooah = water

aguacate (m): ah-gooah-kah-teh = avocado

ahora: ah-oh-rah = now

ahora mismo: ah-hoh-rah mees-moh = right now

ahorrar: ah-hoh-rrahr = to save

ajedrez (m): ah-Heh-drehs = chess

ají (m): ah-Hee = hot pepper (South America)

ajo (m): ah-Hoh = garlic

al fin: ahl feen = finally

alarma (f): ah-lahr-mah = alarm

alcalde (m, f): ahl-kahl-deh = mayor

alegrarse (de): ah-leh-grahr-seh (deh) = to be glad, to be happy

alegre: ah-leh-greh = happy

alegremente: ah-leh-greh-mehn-teh = happily

alemán/alemana (m,f): ah-leh-mahn/nah = German

alfombra (f): ahl-fohm-bvrah = rug

algodón (m): ahl-goh-dohn = cotton

algún: ahl-goon = some

allá: ah-yah = over there

allí: ah-yee = there

almacén (m): ahl-mah-sehn = department store

almorzar (ue): ahl-mohr-sahr = to eat lunch

almuerzo (m): ahl-mooehr-soh = lunch

alrededor de: ahl-reh-deh-dohr de = around

alto: ahl-toh = tall; high

amable: ah-mah-bvleh = nice

amar: ah-mahr = to love

amarillo: ah-mah-ree-yoh = yellow

añadir: ah-nyah-deer = to add

andar: ahn-dahr = to walk

año (m): ah-nyoh = year

antes (de): ahn-tehs (deh) = before

apagar: ah-pah-gahr = to turn off

aparecer: ah-pah-reh-sehr = to appear

aplaudir: ah-plahoo-deer = to applaud

aplicar(se): ah-plee-kahr(seh) = to apply (oneself)

aprender: ah-prehn-dehr = to learn

apresurarse: ah-preh-soo-rahr-seh = to hurry

apretado: ah-preh-tah-doh = tight

aprobar (un examen): ah-proh-bahr (oon ehk-sah-mehn) = to pass
(a test)

aquel, aquella: ah-kehl, ah-keh-yah = that

aquél, aquélla: ah-kehl, ah-keh-yah = that one

aquellos, aquellas: ah-keh-yohs, ah-keh-yahs = those

aquéllos, aquéllas: ah-keh-yohs, ah-keh-yahs = those ones

aquí: ah-kee = here

aretes (m): ah-reh-tehs = earrings

arreglar: ah-rreh-glahr = to repair

arroz (m): ah-rrohs = rice

ascensor (m): ah-sehn-sohr = elevator

asegurarse de: ah-seh-goo-rahr-seh deh = to make sure

asesor/a (m, f): ah-seh-sohr/rah = consultant

asiento (m): ah-seeehn-toh = seat

asistir: ah-sees-teer = to attend

asombrado: ah-sohm-bvrah-doh = astonished, surprised, amazed aspiradora: ahs-pee-rah-doh-rah = vacuum cleaner

asustado: ah-soos-tah-doh = frightened

atacar: ah-tah-kahr = to attack

atentamente: ah-tehn-tah-mehn-teh = sincerely yours

atractivo: ah-trahk-tee-bvoh = attractive

atroz: ah-trohs = atrocious

atún (m): ah-toon = tuna

auditorio (m): ahoo-dee-toh-reeoh = auditorium

aumento (m): ahoo-mehn-toh = raise

aumento de sueldo (m): ahoo-mehn-toh deh sooehl-doh = raise (of salary)

auto (m): ahoo-toh = car (South America)

autopista (f): ahoo-toh-pees-tah = freeway

avenida (f): ah-bveh-nee-dah = avenue

avergonzado: ah-bvehr-gohn-sah-doh = embarrassed, ashamed

avergonzarse de: ah-bvehr-gohn-sahr-seh deh = to be ashamed of

avión (m): ah-bveeohn = plane

ayer: ah-yehr = yesterday

ayudar: ah-yoo-dahr = to help

azul: ah-sool = blue

B

bailar: bvahee-lahr = to dance

bajo: bvah-Ho = short, low, under

balcón (m): bvahl-kohn = balcony

baloncesto (m): bvah-lohn-sehs-toh = basketball

bañar: bvah-nyahr = to bathe (someone)

bañarse: bvah-nyahr-seh = to bathe oneself

bañera (f): bah-nyeh-rah = bathtub

baño (m): bvah-nyoh = bathroom

banquero/a (m, f): bvahn-keh-roh/rah = banker

barco (m): bvahr-koh = boat

barrio (m): bvah-rreeoh = neighborhood

basta: bvahs-tah = enough

bastante: bvahs-tahn-teh = quite; enough

basura (f): bvah-soo-rah = garbage

bate (m): bvah-teh = bat

batir: bvah-teer = to beat, whip, whisk

beber: bveh-bvehr = to drink

bebida (f): bveh-bvee-dah = drink

bello: bveh-yoh = beautiful

besar: bveh-sahr = to kiss

biblioteca (f): bvee-bvleeoh-teh-kah = library

bicicleta (f): bvee-see-kleh-tah = bicycle

bigote (m): bvee-goh-teh = moustache

bistec (m): bvees-tehk = steak

blanco: bvlahn-koh = white

boca (f): bvoh-kah = mouth

boda (f): bvoh-dah = wedding

boleto (m): bvoh-leh-toh = ticket

bolsillo (m): bvohl-see-yoh = pocket

bonito: bvoh-nee-toh = pretty

botella (f): bvoh-teh-yah = bottle

brazo (m): bvrah-soh = arm

brevemente: bvreh-bveh-mehn-teh = briefly

brillo: bvree-yoh = shine

brócoli (m): bvroh-koh-lee = broccoli

bronceador (m): bvrohn-sehah-dohr = suntan lotion

broncearse: bvrohn-seh-ahr-seh = to tan

bueno: bvooeh-noh = good

bulevar (m): bvoo-leh-bvahr = boulevard

burlarse (de): bvoor-lahr-seh (deh) = to make fun of

buscar: bvoos-kahr = to search, to look for

brevemente: bvreh-bveh-mehn-teh = briefly

brillo: bvree-yoh = shine

brócoli (m): bvroh-koh-lee = broccoli

bronceador (m): bvrohn-sehah-dohr = suntan lotion

broncearse: bvrohn-seh-ahr-seh = to tan

bueno: bvooeh-noh = good

---

bulevar (m): bvoo-leh-bvahr = boulevard

burlarse (de): bvoor-lahr-seh (deh) = to make fun of

buscar: bvoos-kahr = to search, to look for

C

caballo (m): kah-bvah-yoh = horse

caber: kah-bvehr = to fit

cabeza (f): kah-bveh-sah = head

caer: cah-ehr = to fall

café (m): kah-feh = coffee

caja (f): kah-Hah = box

cajero/a (m, f): kah-Heh-roh/rah = cashier

caliente: kah-leeehn-teh = hot [temperature]

calificar: kah-lee-fee-kahr = to grade (papers, exams, and so on)

callarse: kah-yahr-seh = to be silent

calle (f): kah-yeh = street

calor (m): kah-lohr = heat

cartero/a (m, f): kahr-teh-roh/rah = postal worker

casa (f): kah-sah = house

casarse: kah-sahr-seh = to get married

cascada (f): kahs-kah-dah = waterfall

casi: kah-see = almost

cebollas (f): seh-bvoh-yahs = onions

cena (f): seh-nah = supper

centro comercial (m): sehn-troh coh-mehr-see-ahl = shopping mall

cepillarse: seh-pee-yahr-seh = to brush (hair, teeth)

cerámica (f): seh-rah-mee-kah = ceramic

cerca (de): sehr-kah (deh) = near (to)

cereales (m): seh-reh-ah-lehs = cereals

cereza (f): seh-reh-sah = cherry

cero (m): seh-roh = zero

cerrado: seh-rrah-doh = closed

cerrar: seh-rrahr = to close

cerveza (f): sehr-bveh-sah = beer

césped (m): sehs-pehd = lawn

champán (m): chahm-pahn = champagne

chaqueta (f): chah-keh-tah = jacket

cheque (m): cheh-keh = check

chico: chee-koh = little; small

chile (m): chee-leh chiste (m): chees-teh = joke

chofer (m): choh-fehr = driver

cielo (m): seeeh-loh = sky

ciencia (f): seeehn-seeah = science

cierto: seeehr-toh = certain, sure

cine (m): see-neh = cinema

ciruela (f): see-roo-eh-lah = plum

cirugía (f): see-roo-Heeah = surgery

cirujano (m): see-roo-hah-noh = surgeon

cita (f): see-tah = appointment, date

ciudad (f): seeoo-dahd = city

claro: klah-roh = light

cobre (m): koh-bvreh = copper

coche (m): koh-cheh = car

cochecito (m): koh-cheh-see-toh = baby carriage

cocina (f): koh-see-nah = kitchen

cocinar: koh-see-nahr = to cook

cocinero/a (m, f): koh-see-neh-rah = cook

coco (m): koh-koh = coconut

código postal (m): koh-dee-goh pohs-tahl = postal code [ZIP code]

coger: koh-hehr = to catch

colgar: kohl-gahr = to hang; to hang up

collar (m): koh-yahr = necklace= hot pepper (Mexico and Guatemala)

colocar: koh-loh-kahr = to place (something)

colocarse: koh-loh-kahr-seh = to place oneself; to get a job

comedor (m): koh-meh-dohr = dining room

comenzar (ie): koh-mehn-sahr = to begin

comer: koh-mehr = to eat

comida (f): koh-mee-dah = dinner

cómo: koh-moh = how

compañero/a (m, f): kohm-pah-nyeh-roh/rah = friend

compartir: kohm-pahr-teer = to share

completamente: kohm-pleh-tah-mehn-teh = completely

comportamiento (m): kohm-pohr-tah-meeehn-toh = behavior

comprar: kohm-prahr = to buy

computadora (f): kohm-poo-tah-doh-rah = computer

computadora portátil (f): lah kohm-poo-tah-doh-rah pohr-tah-teel = laptop computer

concesión (f): kohn-seh-seeohn = dealership

concienzudo: kohn-seeehn-soo-doh = conscientious

concluir: kohn-clueer = to conclude

conducir: kohn-doo-seer = to steer, to drive

confianza (f): kohn-feeahn-sah = confidence

conocer: koh-noh-sehr = to know (to be acquainted with)

conseguir (i): kohn-seh-geer = to get, obtain

consejo (m): kohn-seh-hoh = advice

consentir (ie): kohn-sehn-teer = to consent

construir: kohn-strooeer = to build

contar: kohn-tahr = count

contento: kohn-tehn-toh = content; satisfied

contestar: kohn-tehs-tahr = to answer

continuar: kohn-tee-nooahr = to continue

contratar: kohn-trah-tahr = to hire

contribuir: kohn-tree-booeer = to contribute

convencer: kohn-bvehn-sehr = to convince

conveniente: kohn-bveh-neeehn-teh = fitting

conviene: kohn-bveeeh-neh = it is advisable that

copiar: koh-peeahr = to copy, cheat

corazón (m): koh-rah-sohn = heart

corregir (i): koh-rreh-heer = to correct

correo (m): koh-rreh-oh = mail; post

correo electrónico (m): koh-rreh-oh eh-lehk-troh-nee-koh = e-mail

correr: koh-rrehr = to run

corrida de toros (f): koh-rree-dah deh toh-rohs = bullfight

cortar: kohr-tahr = to cut

cortés (cortesa): kohr-tehs, kohr-teh-sah = courteous

cortesía (f): kohr-teh-seeah = courtesy

cosa (f): koh-sah = thing

costar: kohs-tahr = to cost (as in price)

crecer: kreh-sehr = to grow

creer: kreh-ehr = to disbelieve

crucero (m): kroo-seh-roh = cruise

cuadra (f): kooah-drah = block

cuál(es): kooahl, koo-ah-lehs = which, what

cuándo: kooahn-doh = when

cuánto: kooahn-toh = how much

cuarto (m): kooahr-toh = fourth

cuarto (m): kooahr-toh = quarter

cuarto (m): kooahr-toh = room

cubrir: koobv-reer = to cover

cuchara (f): koo-chah-rah = spoon

cuello (m): kooeh-yoh = neck

cuenta (f): kooehn-tah = account

cuenta bancaria (f): kooehn-tah bvahn-kah-reeah = bank account

cuerpo (m): kooehr-poh = body

cuidado (m): kooee-dah-doh = care

cumpleaños (m): koom-pleeah-nyohs = birthday

cuñada (f): koo-nyah-dah = sister-in-law

cuñado (m): koo-nyah-doh = brother-in-law

curioso: koo-reeoh-soh = curious

D

dar: dahr = to give

dar un paseo: dahr oon pah-sehoh = to take a walk

dato (m): dah-toh = data

de: deh = from

de antemano: deh ahn-teh-mah-noh = beforehand, in advance

de buena gana: deh bvooeh-nah gah-nah = willingly

de nuevo: deh nooeh-bvoh = again

de repente: deh reh-pehn-teh = suddenly

de retraso: deh reh-trah-soh = late (in arriving)

de vez en cuando: deh bvehs ehn kooahn-doh = from time to time

deber: deh-bvehr = to have to

débil: deh-bveel = weak

débito (m): deh-bvee-toh = debit

decidir: deh-see-deer = to decide

décimo (m): deh-see-moh = tenth

decir: deh-seer = to tell, say

dedo (f): deh-doh = finger

dedo del pie (m): deh-doh dehl peeeh = toe

defender: deh-fehn-dehr = to defend

dejar (el trabajo): deh-hahr (ehl trah-bvah-hoh) = to quit (work)

delante (de): deh-lahn-teh (deh) = in front of

delgado: dehl-gah-doh = thin

delicioso: deh-lee-seeoh-soh = delicious

demasiado/a (m, f): deh-mah-seeah-doh/dah = rather, too, too
much

demostrar: deh-mohs-trahr = to demonstrate

dentista (m): dehn-tees-tah = dentist

dentro (de): dehn-troh (deh) = inside (of)

deporte (m): deh-pohr-teh = sport

deportivo: deh-pohr-tee-bvoh = sporty

deprimido: deh-pree-mee-doh = depressed

derecha (f): deh-reh-chah = right

derecho (m): deh-reh-choh = straight

derramar: deh-rrah-mahr = to spill

desafortunadamente: deh-sah-fohr-too-nah-dah-mehn-teh =
unfortunately

desayunarse: deh-sah-yoo-nahr-seh = to have breakfast

desayuno (m): deh-sah-yoo-noh = breakfast

descansar: dehs-kahn-sahr = to rest

desconocido/a (m, f): dehs-kohn-oh-see-doh/dah = stranger

describir: dehs-kree-bveer = to describe

descubrir: dehs-koobv-reer = to discover

descuidado: dehs-kooee-dah-doh = untidy

desde: dehs-deh = from, since

desear: deh-sehahr = to desire, to wish, to want

desenfrenadamente: deh-sehn-freh-nah-dah-mehn-teh = unrestrainedly

desfile (m): dehs-fee-leh = parade

desmayarse: dehs-mah-yahr-seh = to faint

despacio: dehs-pah-seeoh = slowly

despedir(se) (i): dehs-peh-deer (seh) = to say goodbye

despertar(se) (ie): dehs-pehr-tahr (seh) = to wake up

después: dehs-pooehs = after

destruir: dehs-trooeer = to destroy

desvestirse (i): dehs-bvehs-teer-seh = to get undressed

devolver (ue): deh-bvol-bvehr = to return

día (m): deeah = day

diario (m): deeah-reeoh = newspaper

dibujo (m): dee-bvoo-Hoh = drawing; pattern

diccionario (m): deek-seeohn-ah-reeoh = dictionary

diciembre (m): dee-seeehm-bvreh = December

diente (m): deeehn-teh = tooth

difícil: dee-fee-seel = difficult

dinero (m): dee-neh-roh = money

dirección (f): dee-rehk-see-ohn = address

discutir: dees-koo-teer = to discuss, to debate

disponible: dees-poh-nee-bvleh = available

distinguir: dees-teen-geer = to distinguish

distribuir: dees-tree-bvooeer = to distribute

divertido: dee-bvehr-tee-doh = amusing; funny

divertirse (ie): dee-bvehr-teer-seh = to have fun

doblar: doh-bvlahr = to turn

doce: doh-seh = twelve

doler (ue): doh-lehr = to hurt

dolor (m): doh-lohr = pain

dolor de muelas (m): doh-lohr deh mooeh-lahs = toothache

domingo (m): doh-meen-goh = Sunday

¿dónde?: dohn-deh = where

dormir (ue): dohr-meer = to sleep

dormirse (ue): dohr-meer-seh = to fall asleep

dos: dohs = two

ducharse: doo-chahr-seh = to take a shower

duda (f): doo-dah = doubt

dudar: doo-dahr = to doubt

dudoso: doo-doh-soh = doubtful

dulce: dool-seh = sweet

durante: doo-rahn-teh= during

durazno (m): doo-rahs-noh = peach

E

edificio (m): eh-dee-fee-seeoh = building

eficiente: eh-fee-seeehn-teh = efficient

egoísta: eh-gohees-tah = selfish

ejercicio (m): eh-hehr-see-seeoh = exercise

el: ehl = the

él: ehl = he

elegante: eh-leh-gahn-teh = elegant

elegir (i): eh-leh-Heer = to elect

ella: eh-yah = she

ellos, ellas: eh-yohs, eh-yahs = they

embotellada: ehm-bvoh-teh-yah-dah = bottled

emocionado: eh-moh-seeoh-nah-doh = excited

empezar: ehm-peh-sahr = to begin; to start

empleo (m): ehm-pleh-oh = job

empujar: ehm-poo-hahr = to push

en: ehn = in, on, at

en seguida: ehn seh-gee-dah = immediately

en taxi: ehn tahk-see = by taxi

en vez de: ehn vehs deh = instead of

encantado: ehn-kahn-tah-doh = delighted

encantador: ehn-kahn-tah-dohr = enchanting

encender (ie): ehn-sehn-dehr = to light

encontrar: ehn-kohn-trahr = to find

encontrarse (ue): ehn-kohn-trahr-seh = to meet, be located

encuesta (f): ehn-kooehs-tah = survey

enemigo (m): eh-neh-mee-goh = enemy

enero (m): eh-neh-roh = January

enfadado: ehn-fah-dah-doh = angry

enfadar: ehn-fah-dahr = to anger, irritate

enfadarse (con): ehn-fah-dahr-seh (kohn) = to get angry, annoyed (with)

enfermero/a (m, f): ehn-fehr-meh-roh/rah = nurse

enfermo/a (m, f): ehn-fehr-moh = sick person

enfrente (de): ehn-frehn-teh (deh) = in front (of)

engañar: ehn-gah-nyahr = to deceive

engañarse: ehn-gah-nyahr-seh = to be mistaken

enojado: eh-noh-Hah-do = angry, mad

enojarse: eh-noh-Hahr-seh = to become angry

ensalada (f): ehn-sah-lah-dah = salad

enseñar: ehn-seh-nyahr = to teach

entender (ie): ehn-tehn-dehr = to understand

entero (m): ehn-teh-roh = whole

entonces: ehn-tohn-sehs = then

entradas (f): ehn-trah-dahs = hors d'oeuvres

entre: ehn-treh = between

entrenador/a (m, f): ehn-treh-nah-dohr/rah= coach

entrevista (f): ehn-treh-bvees-tah = interview

enviar: ehn-bveeahr = to send

envolver (ue): ehn-bvohl-bvehr (oo-eh) = to wrap up

equipaje (m): eh-kee-pah-Heh = baggage

equipo (m): eh-kee-poh = team

equivocarse: eh-kee-bvoh-kahr-seh = to make a mistake, to be mistaken escaparate (m): ehs-kah-pah-rah-teh = store window

escena (f): ehs-seh-nah = scene

escoger: ehs-koh-hehr = to choose

esconder: ehs-kohn-dehr = to hide (something)

esconder(se): ehs-kohn-dehr(seh) = to hide (oneself)

escribir: ehs-kree-bveer = to write

escritor/a (m, f): ehs-kree-tohr/rah = writer

escuchar: ehs-koo-chahr = to listen; to hear

escuela (f): ehs-kooeh-lah = school

escultura (f): ehs-kool-too-rah = sculpture

ese, esa: eh-seh, eh-sah = that

ése, ésa: eh-seh, eh-sah = that one

esencial: eh-sehn-seeahl = essential

esos, esas: eh-sohs, eh-sahs = those

ésos, ésas: eh-sohs, eh-sahs = those ones

español (m): ehs-pah-nyohl = Spanish (language)

español/a (m, f): ehs-pah-nyohl/ah = Spanish (person)

esparcir: ehs-pahr-seer = to spread out

especial: ehs-peh-seeahl = special

especialmente: ehs-peh-seeahl-mehn-teh = especially

espectáculo (m): eh-spehk-tah-koo-loh = show

esperar: ehs-peh-rahr = to wait, to hope

espinaca (f): ehs-pee-nah-kah = spinach

esposo/a (m, f): ehs-poh-soh/sah = spouse

esquí (m): ehs-kee = ski

esquiar: ehs-keeahr = to ski

esquina (f): ehs-kee-nah = corner

estación (m): ehs-tah-seeohn = station

estacionamiento (m): ehs-tah-seeoh-nah-meeehn-toh = parking

estadio (m): ehs-tah-deeoh = stadium

estado (m): ehs-tah-doh = state

estallar: ehs-tah-yahr = to break out

estar: ehs-tahr = to be

este, esta: ehs-teh, ehs-tah = this

éste, ésta: ehs-teh, ehs-tah = this one

estómago (m): ehs-toh-mah-goh = stomach

estos, estas: ehs-tohs, ehs-tahs = these

éstos, éstas: ehs-tahs = these ones

estrecho: ehs-treh-choh = narrow

estreñimiento (m): ehs-treh-nyee-meeehn-toh = constipation

estupendo: ehs-too-pehn-doh = stupendous

evidente: eh-bvee-dehn-teh = evident

exacto: ehk-sahk-toh = exact

examinar: ehk-sah-mee-nahr = to test, examine

excelente: ehk-seh-lehn-teh = excellent

excesivo: ehk-seh-see-bvoh = excessive

exigir: ehk-see-Heer = to require, to demand

expedir (i): ehks-peh-deer = to dispatch, issue

explicación (f): ehks-plee-kah-seeohn = explanation

explicar: ehks-plee-kahr = to explain

exposición (f): ehks-poh-see-seeohn = exhibit

extraer: ehks-trah-ehr = to extract

extranjero: ehks-trahn-Heh-roh = foreign

extraño: ehks-trah-nyoh = strange

F

fábrica (f): fah-bvree-kah = factory

fácil: fah-seel = easy

falda (f): fahl-dah = skirt

familia (f): fah-mee-leeah = family

famoso: fah-moh-soh = famous

farmacia (f): fahr-mah-seeah = pharmacy

fastidiado: fahs-tee-deeah-doh = bothered

fe (f): feh = faith

febrero (m): feh-bvreh-roh = February

fecha (f): feh-chah = date

felicidad (f): feh-lee-see-dahd = happiness

feliz: feh-lees = happy

feo: feh-oh = ugly

feroz: feh-rohs = ferocious

ferozmente: feh-rohs-mehn-teh = ferociously

festín (m): fehs-teen = feast

fiarse de: feeahr-seh deh = to trust

fideo (m): fee-de-oh = pasta

fiebre (f): feeeh-bvreh = fever

fiesta (f): feeehs-tah = party

fijarse (en): fee-Hahr-seh (ehn) = to notice

finalmente: fee-nahl-mehn-teh = finally

firmar: feer-mahr = to sign

físico: fee-see-koh = physical

flaco: flah-koh = skinny

flojera (f): floh-Heh-rah = weakness, laziness

flojo: floh-Hoh = loose, slack, lazy

folleto (m): foh-yeh-toh = brochure

fortaleza (f): fohr-tah-leh-sah = fort

fotografiar: foh-toh-grah-feeahr = to photograph

fotógrafo/a (m, f): foh-toh-grah-foh/fah = photographer

franqueza: frah-keh-sah = frankness

frecuentemente: freh-kooehn-teh-mehn-teh = frequently

fresa (f): freh-sah = strawberry (Mexico, Central America, and Spain)

fresco: frehs-koh = cool

frío: freeoh = cold

fruta (f): froo-tah = fruit

frutilla (f): froo-tee-yah = strawberry (from Colombia to the South Pole)

fuera: fooeh-rah = outside

furioso: foo-reeoh-soh = furious

fútbol (m): foot-bvohl = soccer

G

gabinete (m): gah-bvee-neh-teh = cabinet (government)

galletas (f): gah-yeh-tahs = cookies; crackers

ganar: gah-nahr = to earn, win

ganga (f): gahn-gah = bargain

ganso (m): gan-soh = goose

garantía (f): gah-rahn-teeah = warranty

garganta (f): gahr-gahn-tah = throat

gastar: gah-stahr = to spend

gastos (m): gahs-tohs = expenses

gato (m): gah-toh = cat

generoso: Heh-neh-roh-soh = generous

genial: Heh-neeahl = pleasant

gerente (m, f): Heh-rehn-teh = manager

gimnasio (m): Heem-nah-seeoh = gym

globo (m): gloh-bvoh = balloon, globe

gordo: gohr-doh = fat

grabación (f): grah-bvah-seeohn = tape recording

gracias: grah-seeahs = thank you

grande: grahn-deh = big; large

gris: grees = grey

gritar: gree-tahr = to scream

guantera (f): gooahn-teh-rah = glove compartment

guapo: gooah-poh = pretty, good-looking

guayaba (f): gooah-yah-bvah = guava

guerra (f): geh-rrah = war

guía (m, f) gheeah = guide

guiar: gee-ahr = to guide

guisante (m): gee-sahn-teh = pea

gustar: goos-tahr = to like

H

habituar: ah-bvee-tooahr = to accustom

hablador: ah-bvlah-dohr = talkative

hablar: ah-bvlahr = to talk, speak

hace (+ time): ah-seh = ago

hacer ejercicio: ah-sehr eh-Hehr-see-seeoh = to exercise

hacer: ah-sehr = to make, to do

hacerse: ah-sehr-seh = to become

hambre: ahm-bvreh = hunger

hay: ahy = there is, are

hecho a mano: eh-choh ah mah-noh = hand made

helado (m): eh-lah-doh = ice cream

helar (ie): eh-lahr = to freeze

herencia (f): ehr-ehn-seeah = inheritance

hermana (f): ehr-mah-nah = sister

hermano (m): ehr-mah-noh = brother

hígado (m): ee-gah-doh = liver

higo (m): ee-goh = fig

hija (f): ee-Hah = daughter

hijo (m): ee-Hoh = son

hijos (m): ee-Hohs = children

hombre (m): ohm-bvreh = man

hombro (m): ohm-bvroh = shoulder

hora (f): oh-rah = hour

horrible: hoh-rree-bvleh = horrible

hospedar: ohs-peh-dahr = to house

hoy: ohy = today

hoy (en) día: ohy (ehn) deeah = nowadays

huachinango (m): ooah-chee-nahn-goh = red snapper

hueso (m): ooeh-soh = bone

huéspedes (m): ooehs-peh-dehs = guests

huevo (m): ooeh-bvoh = egg

I

identificación (f): ee-dehn-tee-fee-kah-seeohn = identification

idioma (m): ee-deeoh-mah = language

iglesia (f): ee-gleh-seeah = church

imperativo: eem-peh-rah-tee-bvoh = imperative

impermeable (m): eem-pehr-meh-ah-bleh = raincoat

importante: eem-pohr-tahn-teh = important

imposible: eem-poh-see-bvleh = impossible

imprimir: eem-pree-meer = to print

improbable: eem-proh-bvah-bvleh = improbable

impuesto (m): eem-pooehs-toh = tax

incluido: een-klooee-doh = included

incluir: een-klooeer = to include

increíble: een-krehee-bvleh = incredible

indispensable: een-dees-pehn-sah-bvleh = indispensable

infeliz: een-feh-lees = unhappy

ingeniero/a (m, f): een-Heh-neeeh-roh/rah = engineer

inglés (m): een-glehs = English (language)

inglés/a (m, f): een-glehs/ah = English (person)

ingrediente (m): een-greh-deeehn-teh = ingredient

ingresar: een-greh-sahr = to deposit

injusto: een-Hoo-stoh = unfair

inmigración (f): een-mee-grah-seeohn = immigration

inodoro: ee-noh-doh-roh = without a smell

insistir: een-sees-teer = to insist

institución de beneficencia (f): een-stee-too-seeohn deh bveh-neh-fee-sehn-seeah = charity organization

inteligente: een-teh-lee-Hehn-teh = intelligent

interesante: een-teh-reh-sahn-teh = interesting

intestino (m): een-tehs-tee-noh = bowel; intestine; gut

invierno (m): een-bveeeehr-noh = winter

ir: eer = to go

ir de compras: eer deh kohm-prahs = to go shopping

irónico: ee-roh-nee-koh = ironic

irritado: ee-rree-tah-doh = irritated

irse: eer-seh = to go away

isla (f): ees-lah = island

izquierda: ees-keeehr-dah = left

J

jardín (m): Hahr-deen = garden

jarrón (m): Hah-rrohn = vase

jefe (m): Heh-feh = boss

joven: Hoh-bvehn = young

jueves (m): Hooeh-bvehs = Thursday

juez (m, f): Hooehs = judge

jugar (ue): Hoo-gahr = to play

jugar (ue) a las damas: Hoo-gahr ah lahs dah-mahs = to play checkers

jugo (m): Hoo-goh = juice

juguete (m): Hoo-geh-teh = toyjulio (m): Hoo-leeoh = July

junio (m): Hoo-neeoh = June

junto: Hoon-toh = together

justo: Hoos-toh = fair

juzgar: Hoos-gahr = to judge

L

la: lah = the; her, it

ladrar: lah-drahr = to bark

lago (m): lah-goh = lake

lamentable: lah-mehn-tah-bvleh = regrettable

lamentar: lah-mehn-tahr = to regret

lana (f): lah-nah = wool

langostino (m): lahn-gohs-tee-noh = prawn

lápiz (m): lah-pees = pencil

largo: lahr-goh = long

las: lahs = the; them

lástima (f): lahs-tee-mah = pity; shame

lavar: lah-bvahr = to wash

lavarse: lah-bvahr-seh = to wash oneself

le: leh = to him, to her, to you formal

leal: leh-ahl = loyal

lección (f): lehk-seeohn = lesson

leche (f): leh-cheh = milk

lechuga (f): leh-choo-gah = lettuce

leer: leh-ehr = to read

lejos: leh-Hohs = far

lentamente: lehn-tah-mehn-teh = slowly

les: lehs = to them, to you plural

___

levantar: leh-bvahn-tahr = to raise (something)

levantarse: leh-bvahn-tahr-seh = to get up

ley (f): leh = law

libra (f): lee-bvrah = pound

libre: lee-bvreh = free

libro (m): lee-bvroh = book

ligero: lee-Heh-roh = light, swift

limón (m): lee-mohn = lemon

limpiar: leem-peeahr = to clean

línea (f): lee-neh-ah = line

lisonjeado: lee-sohn-Heh-ah-doh = flattered

listo: lees-toh = ready

llamar: yah-mahr = to call

llamarse: yah-mahr-seh = to be called, to call oneself

llave (f): yah-bveh = key

llegar: yeh-gahr = to arrive

llevar: yeh-bvahr = to wear

llorar: yoh-rahr = to cry

llover (ue): yoh-bvehr = to rain

lluvia (f): yoo-bveeah = rain

lo: loh = him, it

lodo (m): loh-doh = mud

los: lohs = the, them

luego: looeh-goh = later

lugar (m): loo-ghar = place

lujoso: loo-Hoh-soh = luxurious

luna (f): loo-nah = moon

lunes (m): loo-nehs = Monday

M

madera (f): mah-deh-rah = wood

madre (f): mah-dreh = mother

madrina (f): mah-dree-nah = godmother

magnífico: mahg-nee-fee-koh = magnificent

maleta (f): mah-leh-tah = luggage; suitcase

malo: mah-loh = bad

mañana (f): mah-nyah-nah = morning

mañana (f): mah-nyah-nah = tomorrow

mandar: mahn-dahr = to command, to order, to send

manejar: mah-neh-Hahr = to drive, to operate, to manage

manga (f): mahn-gah = sleeve

mango (m): mahn-goh = mango

mantel (m): mahn-tehl = tablecloth

mantequilla (f): mahn-teh-kee-yah = butter

manzana (f): mahn-sah-nah = apple

mapa (m): mah-pah = map

maquillarse: mah-kee-yahr-seh = to put on makeup

máquina (f): mah-kee-nah = machine

mar (m): mahr = sea

maravilloso: mah-rah-bvee-yoh-soh = marvelous

marcar: mahr-kahr = to mark; to dial; to punch in the number

marcharse: mahr-chahr-seh = to go away

marea (f): mah-reh-ah = tide

mareo (m): mah-reh-oh = dizziness

maridos (m): mah-ree-dohs = married couple

mariposa (f): mah-ree-poh-sah = butterfly

marisco (m): mah-rees-koh = seafood

marrón: mah-rrohn = brown

martes (m): mahr-tehs = Tuesday

marzo (m): mahr-soh = March

más: mahs = more

más tarde: mahs tahr-deh = later

masticar: mahs-tee-kahr = to chew

materialista: mah-teh-reeah-lees-tah = materialistic

matrícula (f): mah-tree-koo-lah = tuition

mayo (m): mah-yoh = Mayme: meh = me, to me

medicina (f): meh-dee-see-nah = medicine

médico/a (m, f): meh-dee-koh/kah = physician; doctor

medio (m): meh-deeoh = half

medio baño (m): meh-deeoh bvah-nyoh = half-bathroom (a bathroom with no shower or tub)

mediodía (m): meh-deeoh-dee-ah = noon

medir (i): meh-deer = to measure

mejor: meh-Hohr = best

melón (m): meh-lohn = melon

memorizar: meh-moh-ree-sahr = to memorize

menos: meh-nohs = less

mensajero/a (m, f): mehn-sah-Heh-roh/rah = messenger

mentir: mehn-teer = to lie

merecer: meh-reh-sehr = to deserve

mes (m): mehs = month

mesa (f): meh-sah = table

metro (m): meh-troh = subway

mezclar: mehs-klahr = to mix

mi(s): mee(s) = my

mientras: meeehn-trahs = while

miércoles (m): meeehr-koh-lehs = Wednesday

mil (m): meel = one thousand

milla (f): mee-yah = milemillón (m): mee-yohn = one million

minuto (m): mee-noo-toh = minute

mío/a(s) (m, f, pl.): mee-oh(s)/ah(s) = mine

mirar: mee-rahr = to look at, to watch

mismo: mees-moh = same

mochila (f): moh-chee-lah = backpack

moda (f): moh-dah = style

moderno: moh-dehr-noh = modern

mojado: moh-Hah-doh = wet

moneda (f): moh-neh-dah = coin

montaña (f): mohn-tah-nyah = mountain

mora (f): moh-rah = blackberry

morado: moh-rah-doh = purple

moreno: moh-reh-noh = dark-haired

morir (ue): moh-reer = to die

---

mostaza: mohs-tah-sah = mustard

mostrar (ue): mohs-trahr = to show

mucho: moo-choh = a lot; much

mueble (m): mooeh-bvleh = furniture

mujer (f): moo-Hehr = woman

muñeca (f): moo-nyeh-kah = wrist

muñeco de nieve (m): moo-nyeh-koh deh neeeh-bveh = snowman

museo (m): moo-seh-oh = museummúsica clásica (f): moo-see-kah

klah-see-kah = classical music

muslo (m): moos-loh = thigh

muy: mooee = very

N

nacer: nah-sehr = to be born

nada: nah-dah = nothing

nadar: nah-dahr = to swim

nadie: nah-deeeh = nobody, no one

naipe (m): nahee-peh = card (playing)

naranja (f): nah-rahn-Hah = orange

nariz (f): nah-rees = nose

natación (f): nah-tah-seeohn = swimming

natural: nah-too-rahl = natural

necesario: neh-seh-sah-reeoh = necessary

necesitar: neh-seh-see-tahr = to need

negar (ie): neh-gahr = to deny

negro: neh-groh = black

nevar (ie): neh-bvahr = to snow

ni . . . ni: nee . . . nee = neither . . . nor

nieta (f): neeeh-tah = granddaughter

nieto (m): neeeh-toh = grandson

niña (f): nee-nyah = girl

ningún: neen-goon = none

niño (m): nee-nyoh = boy

no: noh = no, not

noche (f): noh-cheh = night

nos: nohs = us, to us, ourselves

nosotros: noh-soh-trohs = we, us

noticias (f): noh-tee-seeahs = news

novela (f): noh-bveh-lah = novel

noveno: noh-bveh-noh = ninth

noviembre (m): noh-bveeehm-bvreh = November

novio/a (m,f): noh-bveeoh/ah = boyfriend/girlfriend

nube (f): noo-bveh = cloud

nuera (f): nooeh-rah = daughter-in-law

nuestro/a (s): nooehs-troh(s)/trah(s) = our (ours)

nuevo: nooeh-bvoh = new

número (m): noo-meh-roh = number

nunca: noon-kah = never

O

o: oh = or

obedecer: oh-bveh-deh-sehr = to obey

obvio: ohb-bveeoh = obvious

octavo: ohk-tah-bvoh = eighth

octubre (m): ohk-too-bvreh = October

ocupado: oh-koo-pah-doh = occupied; busy

ofrecer: oh-freh-sehr = to offer, give

oír: oheer = to hear

ojalá que . . .: oh-Hah-lah keh = if only . . .

ojo (m): oh-Hoh = eye

oler: oh-lehr = to smell

olla (f): oh-yah = pot

olvidar: ohl-bvee-dahr = to forget

olvidarse (de): ohl-bvee-dahr-seh (deh)= to forget about

once: ohn-seh = eleven

oponer: oh-poh-nehr = to oppose

optimista: ohp-tee-mees-tah = optimistic

ordenar: ohr-deh-nahr = to order (command)

ordinario: ohr-dee-nah-reeoh = ordinary

oreja (f): oh-reh-Hah = ear

---

orgulloso: ohr-goo-yoh-soh = proud

orina (f): oh-ree-nah = urine

oro (m): oh-roh = gold

os: ohs = you, to you, yourselves

oscuro: ohs-koo-roh = dark

otoño (m): oh-toh-nyoh = autumn

otro: oh-troh = another

P

paciencia (f): pah-seeehn-seeah = patience

padre (m): pah-dreh = father

padrino (m): pah-dree-noh = godfather

pagado: pah-gah-doh = paid for

pagar: pah-gahr = to pay

país (m): pahees = country

pájaro (m): pah-Hah-roh = bird

palabra (f): pah-lah-bvrah = word

palomitas de maíz (f): pah-loh-mee-tahs deh mahees = popcorn

panadero/a (m, f): pah-nah-deh-roh/rah = baker

pantalla (f): pahn-tah-yah = screen

pantalones (m): pahn-tah-loh-nehs = trousers

pantorrilla (f): pahn-toh-rree-yah = calf

papas (f): pah-pahs = potatoes

papas fritas (f): pah-pahs free-tahs = potato chips

papaya (f): pah-pah-yah = papaya

papel (m): pah-pehl = paper, role

paquete (m): pah-keh-teh = package

para: pah-rah = for

parar: pah-rahr = to stop (something)

pararse: pah-rahr-seh = to stop oneself

parecer: pah-reh-sehr = to seem

parque (m): pahr-keh = park

partido (m): pahr-tee-doh = (sports) gamepasado: pah-sah-doh = past, last

pasaporte (m): pah-sah-pohr-teh = document; paper; passport

pasar: pah-sahr = to spend (time)

pasearse: pah-sehahr-seh = to go for a walk

paseo (m): pah-seh-oh = walk

pasillo (m): pah-see-yoh = aisle

pastel (m): pahs-tehl = cake

patín: pah-teen= skate

pato (m): pah-toh = duck

peaje (m): peh-ah-Heh = toll

pecho (m): peh-choh = chest

pedir (i): peh-deer = to ask for

peinarse: peh-nahr-seh = to comb one's hair

pelar: peh-lahr = to peel

pelea (f): peh-leh-ah = fight

película (f): peh-lee-koo-lah = movie, film

peligroso: peh-lee-groh-soh = dangerous

pelo (m): peh-loh = hair

pensar: pehn-sahr = to think

peor: peh-ohr = worse

pequeño: peh-keh-nyoh = small

pera (f): peh-rah = pear

perder: pehr-dehr = to lose

perezoso: peh-reh-soh-soh = lazy

perfeccionar: pehr-fehk-seeoh-nahr = to perfect

perfecto: pehr-fehk-toh = perfect

periódico (m): peh-reeoh-dee-koh = newspaper

perla (f): pehr-lah = pearl

permitir: pehr-mee-teer = to permit

pero: peh-roh = but

perro (m): peh-rroh = dog

pescado (m): pehs-kah-doh = fish (to eat)

pescar: pehs-kahr = to fish

pesimista: peh-see-mees-tah = pessimistic

peso: peh-soh = weight

pez (m): pehs = fish (live)

---

picante: pee-kahn-teh = hot [flavor]

pie (m): peeeh = foot

pierna (f): peeehr-nah = leg

piloto/a (m,f): pee-loh-toh/tah = pilot

piña (f): pee-nyah = pineapple

pintar: peen-tahr = to paint

pintura (f): peen-too-rah = painting

piscina (f): pees-see-nah = swimming pool

piso (m): pee-soh = floor

planchar: plahn-chahr = to iron

plátano (m): plah-tah-noh = baplato (m): plah-toh = plate

platos (m): plah-tohs = dishes

playa (f): plah-yah = beach

plaza (f): plah-sah = square

plomo (m): ploh-moh = lead

pobre: poh-bvreh = poor

poco (m): poh-koh = a bit; a small amount

poder (ue): poh-dehr = to be able to, can

pollo (m): poh-yoh = chicken

polvo (m): pohl-bvoh = dust

poner (la mesa): poh-nehr (lah meh-sah) = to set (the table)

ponerse: poh-nehr-seh = to put (something on), to become, to place oneself

popular: poh-poo-lahr = popular

por: pohr = for, per

por ciento: pohr seeehn-toh = percent

por consiguiente: pohr kohn-see-geeehn-teh = consequently

por favor: pohr fah-bvohr = please

¿por qué?: pohr keh = why

por supuesto: pohr soo-pooehs-toh = of course

porcentaje (m): pohr-sehn-tah-Heh = percentage

porción (f): pohr-seeohn = portion

porque: pohr-keh = becausenanaposible: poh-see-bvleh = possible

potable: poh-tah-bvleh = drinkable

precio (m): preh-seeoh = price

precioso: preh-seeoh-soh = gorgeous; beautiful; lovely

preferible: preh-feh-ree-bvleh = preferable

preferir (ie): preh-feh-reer = to prefer

preguntar: preh-goon-tahr = to ask (a question)

preocuparse (de): preoh-koo-pahr-seh (deh) = to worry (about)

presión sanguínea (f): preh-seeohn sahn-gee-neh-ah = blood pressure

prestar: preh-stahr = to borrow

prestar atención: prehs-tahr ah-tehn-seeohn = to pay attention

prima (f): pree-mah = cousin [female]

primavera (f): pree-mah-bveh-rah = spring

primero: pree-meh-roh = first

primo (m): pree-moh = cousin [male]

probable: proh-bvah-bvleh = probable

probador (m): proh-bvah-dohr = fitting room

probar(se): proh-bvahr(seh) = to try (on)

producir: proh-doo-seer = to produce

producto lácteo (m): proh-dook-toh lahk-tehoh = dairy product

profundamente: pro-foon-dah-mehn-teh = deeply

prohibir: proh-hee-bveer = to forbid

prometer: proh-meh-tehr = to promise

pronto: prohn-toh = right away, soon

pronunciar: proh-noon-seeahr = to pronounce

propietario/a (m, f): proh-peeeh-tah-reeoh/ah = proprietor, owner

propio: proh-peeoh = [one's] own

próximo: prohk-see-moh = next

proyecto (m): proh-yehk-toh = project

puerto (m): pooehr-toh = port

puesto (m): pooehs-toh = job, position

pulir: poo-leer = to polish

pulmón (m): pool-mohn = lung

pura: poo-rah = pure

Q

que: keh = that, than

¿qué?: keh = what

quedarse: keh-dahr-seh = to stay

quejarse (de): keh-hahr-seh (deh) = to complain (of, about)

quemadura (f): keh-mah-doo-rah = burn

queso (m): keh-soh = cheese

¿quién?: keeehn = who, whom

química (f): kee-mee-kah = chemistry

quinto: keen-toh = fifth

quitar(se): keeh-tahr(seh) = to remove, to take off

R

receta (f): reh-seh-tah = prescription, recipe

recibo (m): reh-see-bvoh = receipt

reclamar: reh-klah-mahr = to demand

recordar: reh-kohr-dahr = to remember

reembolsar: reh-ehm-bvol-sahr = to refund

refresco (m): reh-frehs-koh = soft drink

refriarse: reh-freeahr-seh = to catch a cold

regalo (m): reh-gah-loh = gift

régimen (m): reh-gee-mehn = diet

regla (f): reh-glah = rule, ruler

reglamentos (m, pl.): rehg-lah-mehn-tohs = regulations

regresar: reh-greh-sahr = to return

reino (m): rehee-noh = kingdom

reír: reheer = to laugh

relámpagos: reh-lahm-pah-gohs = lightning

repetir: reh-peh-teer = to repeat

reservación (f): reh-sehr-bvah-seeohn = reservation

responder: rehs-pohn-dehr = to answer

respuesta (f): rehs-pooehs-tah = answer

restaurante (m): rehs-tahoo-rahn-teh = restaurant

retiro: reh-tee-roh = withdrawal

reunión (f): rehoo-neeohn = meeting

reunirse: rehoo-neer-seh = to meet

riñón (m): ree-nyohn = kidney

río (m): ree-oh = river

robar: roh-bvahr = to steal; to rob

robo (m): roh-bvoh = robbery

rojo: roh-Hoh = red

romper: rohm-pehr = to break

rosado: roh-sah-doh = pink

roto: roh-toh = broken, shattered

rótulo (m): roh-too-loh = label

ruido (m): rooee-doh = noise

ruinas (f): rooee-nahs = ruins

ruta (f): roo-tah = road, route

S

sábado (m): sah-bvah-doh = Saturday

saco (m): sah-koh = bag

sagaz: sah-gahs = astute, wise

sala (f): sah-lah = living room

salado: sah-lah-doh = salty

saldo (m): sahl-doh = balance

salir: sah-leer = to leave

saltar: sahl-tahr = to jump

saludable: sah-loo-dah-bvleh = healthy

sandía (f): sahn-dee-ah = watermelon

sangre (f): sahn-greh = blood

secar(se): seh-kahr(seh) = to dry (oneself)

seco: seh-koh = dry

sed: sehd = thirst

seda (f): seh-dah = silk

seguir: seh-gheer = to follow

segundo (m): seh-goon-doh = second

selva (f): sehl-bvah = rainforest

semana (f): seh-mah-nah = week

señal (f): seh-nyahl = sign

señalar: seh-nyah-lahr = to signal

sentir (ie): sehn-teer = to be sorry, to regret

septiembre (m): sehp-teeehm-breh = September

séptimo: sehp-tee-moh = seventh

ser: sehr = to be

sexto: sehks-toh = sixth

siempre: seeehm-preh = always

siguiente: see-geeehn-teh = next

sirviente/a (m, f): seer-bveeehn-teh/tah = servant

sol (m): sohl = sun

sonar (ue): soh-nahr = to ring

sorprendido: sohr-prehn-dee-doh = surprised

sorpresa (f): sohr-preh-sah = surprise

subterráneo: soobv-teh-rrah-neh-oh = underground

suelo (m): sooeh-loh = ground

suelto: sooehl-toh = loose

suerte (f): sooehr-teh = luck

suéter (m): sooeh-tehr = sweater

suficiente: soo-fee-seeehn-teh = enough

sugerir (ie): soo-Heh-reer = to suggest

supermercado (m): soo-pehr-mehr-kah-doh = supermarket

suprimir: soo-pree-meer = to suppress

T

tabla (f): tah-bvlah = board [wood]

tal vez: tahl bvehs = perhaps

talla (f): tah-yah = size (of a person)

tamaño (m): tah-mah-nyoh = size (of a place or object)

también: tahm-bveeehn = also, too

tampoco: tahm-poh-koh = neither; not . . . either

tarde (f): tahr-deh = afternoon, late

tarjeta (f): tahr-Heh-tah = card

teatro (m): teh-ah-troh = theater

teclado (m): teh-klah-doh = keyboard

tele (f): teh-leh = TV (colloquial)

televisión (f): teh-leh-bvee-seeohn = television

tempestad (f): tehm-pehs-tahd = storm

temprano: tehm-prah-noh = early

tener (ie): teh-nehr = to have

tercero: tehr-seh-roh = third

terminar: tehr-mee-nahr = to finish

tía (f): tee-ah = aunt

tiempo (m): teeehm-poh = time

tiempo (m): teeehm-poh = weather

tienda (f): teeehn-dah = store

tierra (f): teeeh-rrah = land

timbre (m): teem-breh = bell

tintorería (f): teen-toh-reh-reeah = dry cleaner

tío (m): teeoh = uncle

típica: tee-pee-kah = typical

título (m): tee-too-loh = degree

tobillo (m): toh-bvee-yoh = ankle

todavía: toh-dah-bvee-ah = yet; still

todos (los domingos): toh-dohs (lohs doh-meen-gohs) = every (Sunday)

tomar el sol: toh-mahr ehl sohl = to sunbathe

toronja (f): toh-rohn-Hah = grapefruit

torpe: tohr-peh = clumsy

tos (f): tohs = cough

trabajador: trah-bvah-Hah-dohr = hard-working

traducir: trah-doo-seer = to translate

traer: trah-ehr = to bring

tráfico (m): trah-fee-koh = traffic

tragar: trah-gahr = to swallow

traje de baño (m): tra-Heh deh bvah-nyoh = swimsuit

tranquilo: trahn-kee-loh = quiet

tratar de: trah-tahr deh = to try to

tren (m): trehn = train

tronar (ue): troh-nahr = to thunder

trozo (m): troh-soh = piece

trucha (f): troo-chah = trout

truenos (m): trooeh-nohs = thunder

U

un rato: oon rah-toh = awhile

uniforme (m): oo-nee-fohr-meh = uniform

uva (f): oo-bvah = grape

V

vaciar: bvah-seeahr = to empty

valer: bvah-lehr = to be worth

vecindario (m): bveh-seen-dah-reeoh = neighborhood

vehículo (m): bveh-ee-koo-loh = vehicle

vender: bvehn-dehr = to sell

venir: bveh-neer = to come

venta (f): bvehn-tah = sale

ver: bvehr = to see

verano (m): bveh-rah-noh = summer

verdad (f): bvehr-dahd = truth

verde: bvehr-deh = green

vestir (i): bvehs-teer = to clothe

viajar: bveeah-Hahr = to travel

viaje (m): bveeah-Heh = trip

viajero/a (m,f): bveeah-Heh-roh/rah = traveler

vida (f): bvee-dah = life

vidrio (m): bvee-dreeoh = glass

viernes (m): bveeeehr-nehs = Friday

vino (m): bvee-noh = wine

violeta: bveeoh-leh-tah = violet; purple

violín (m): bveeoh-leen = violin

víspera (f): bvees-peh-rah = eve

vivir: bvee-bveer = to live

volar: bvoh-lahr = to fly

volver (ue): bvohl-bvehr = to return

votar: bvoh-tahr = to vote

vuelta (f): bvooehl-tah = lap

vuelto (m): bvooehl-toh = change (as in money back)

Y

ya: yah = already

yerno (m): yehr-noh = son-in-law

Z

zanahoria (f): sah-nah-oh-reeah = carrot

Idioms, Sayings, Modisms & Proverbs

It is a well-known fact that every language has a rich history behind it. Thus, forming different structures to the extent that a group of words' meanings is different from it usually means. This is true in idiomatic expressions, saying, modisms and proverbs. It usually takes years in a country to master their idioms and expressions. However, this chapter is going to give you a walk through it.

- ABRIR(SE) DE CAPA - To speak frankly and sincerely

Se abrió de capa cuando le pregunté acerca de mi hijo. (He gave it to me straight when I asked him about my son.)

- Aguantar carros y carretas - To have the capacity to take a lot of negative acts or nonsense from

A veces tengo que aguantarles carros y carretas a los latosos de mis parientes. (Sometimes I have to take a lot of nonsense from my annoying relatives.)

- Alborotar el gallinero - To get everyone in an uproar

No vayas a decir nada de los despidos proyectados. No queremos alborotar el gallinero. (Don't say anything about the projected layoffs. We don't want to get everyone in an uproar.)

- Aliviar(se) - To give birth

En este hospital se alivió Jimena. (Jimena gave birth in this hospital.)

- Andar - To be after

Enrique anda tras Lucía. (Enrique is after Lucy.)

- Andar amolado(a) - To be in a bad way (as concerns money or health)

He andado amolado de dinero. (I've been in a bad way as concerns money.)

- Andar con el Jesús en la boca - To be distraught

La pobre Leonor anda con el Jesús en la boca. (Poor Leonor is distraught.)

- Andar(se) con rodeos - To beat around the bush

No te andes con rodeos. ¡Dímelo claro! (Don't beat around the bush. Come right out with it!)

- Andar de boca en boca - To go from mouth to mouth, To be on everyone's lips; to be the talk of the town.)

Angélica anda de boca en boca. (Angelica is the talk of the town.)

- Andar de la ceca a la meca; Andar del tingo al tango - To go to a lot of places

Anduve de la ceca a la meca para encontrar lo que quería. (I had to go to a million places to find what I wanted.)

- Andar de malas - To have a run of bad luck

No quiero correr riesgos ahorita. He andado de malas. (I don't want to take any chances. I have had a run of bad luck.)

- Andar (estar) en las nubes - To be in the clouds, To be on cloud nine; to be (mentally) somewhere else (daydreaming)

Desde que lo aceptó Adriana, José Luis anda en las nubes. (Jose Luis has been on cloud nine ever since Adriana agreed to go steady with him.) ¡Muchacho! Atiende a la clase. ¡Estás en las nubes! (Hey, kid! Pay attention in class! You are daydreaming!)

- Andar giro(a) (girito(a)) - To be still going strong

A sus ochenta y siete años, nuestra abuela todavía anda muy girita. (Our grandmother is still going strong at 87.)

- Andar norteado(a) - To be disoriented

Todavía ando norteado. Apenas llevo dos días en esta ciudad. (I'm still disoriented. I've only been in this city for two days.)

- Armar(se) la gorda - To start a fight

Se puso agresivo y armó la gorda en el bar. (He got nasty and started a fight in the bar.)
Si nos siguen provocando, aquí se va a armar la gorda. (If they keep picking on us, there's going to be a fight.)

- Barajar(la) (más) despacio - To shuffle more slowly, To explain more slowly.

Perdón, no entiendo nada. Barájamela más despacio. (Sorry, I didn't get that. Explain it again more slowly.)

- Brillar por su ausencia - To shine by your absence, To be very conspicuously absent

En la boda, Dolores brilló por su ausencia. (Everybody noticed that Dolores wasn't at the wedding.)

- Buscarle ruido al chicharrón - To poke the chicharon until it makes a noise
- Buscarle tres pies al gato - To ask for it; To burn the candle at both ends; To look for trouble

Si no sigues las reglas de esta casa, le estás buscando ruido al chicharrón (le estás buscando tres pies al gato). (If you don't follow the rules of the house, you are looking for trouble.)
Caer al pelo - To be just the thing; to be just what one wants or needs
El cinturón que me regalaste me cayó al pelo. (The belt you gave me was just what I wanted.)

- Caer bien (o mal)* - To like

Elisa me cae muy bien. (I really like Elisa.)
Arturo no me cae bien (Arturo me cae mal). (I don't like Arturo.)
When one is speaking of food, this expression means "it goes down well." When mal is used instead of bien, the meaning is the opposite.
El chocolate me cae mal. (Chocolate doesn't agree with me.)

El consomé le cae bien a uno cuando está enfermo. (Broth goes down well when one is sick.)

Note: In English, the subject used with the verb "to like" is the person who experiences the feeling of liking or affection. In Spanish, the subject is the person who is the object of that liking or affection.

- Caer como cubeta de agua fría - To fall on like a bucket of cold water, To astonish; to stun

La noticia me cayó como cubeta de agua fría. (The news stunned me.)

- Calentar(le) la cabeza a - To heat up 's head, To prejudice against

Efrén le calentó la cabeza a Carlos para que acusara a José. Efren got Carlos all worked up so he would accuse Jose.

- Cargar con el muerto - To carry the body, To be blamed for

Arnulfo tuvo que cargar con el muerto por lo que pasó en la fiesta. (Arnulfo got all the blame for what happened at the party.)

- Chupar(se) el dedo - To suck your thumb, To be born yesterday

No me vengas con ese cuento. No me chupo el dedo, ¿sabes? (Don't give me that story. I wasn't born yesterday, you know.)

- Comer ansias - To eat anxiety, To be anxious or fidgety

No hay prisa. Tómalo con calma. No comas ansias. (There is no hurry. Take it easy. Calm down.)
Por andar comiendo ansias, me salió todo mal. (Everything went wrong because I was in such a nervous state.)

- Comer(se) con los ojos a - To stare longingly at

Juan se la estaba comiendo con los ojos. (Juan was staring at her longingly.)

- Correr como reguero de pólvora - To spread like a trail of burning gunpowder, To spread like wildfire; to travel like lightning

La noticia corrió como reguero de pólvora. (The news spread like wildfire.)

- Correr por cuenta de - To be on, To see to it that ...

Las siguientes copas corren por mi cuenta. (The next round is on me.)

De mi cuenta corre que no lograrán embargarte. (I'll see to it that you're not sued.)

- Costar (mucho) trabajo (see Dar trabajo) - To be very difficult

Me costó mucho trabajo ser amable con Julio. (It was very difficult to speak to Julio politely.)

- Creer(se) la divina garza - To consider yourself the divine stork, To think a lot of yourself; to be conceited

Elena se cree la divina garza porque la escogieron para hacer el comercial. (Elena thinks she's God's gift to this world because she was chosen to do the commercial.)

- Creer(se) la gran cosa - To think a lot of oneself; to be conceited

Chucho se cree la gran cosa porque está en el equipo. (Chucho has a big head because he's on the team. Dar a luz)

- Dar(le) al clavo - To hit the nail on the head

Aurelio le dio al clavo con su respuesta. (Aurelio hit the nail on the head with his answer.)

- Dar(le) ánimo(s) a - To give moral support or courage, To encourage

El güisquito me dio ánimo para entrar a hablar con el director. That whiskey gave me the courage to go in and talk to the director.

Speaker A:

¿Cómo puedes seguir manejando después del accidente?

How can you go on driving after the accident?

Speaker B:

Gracias a Gloria, que siempre me da ánimos.

Thanks to Gloria. She always encourages me and makes me feel brave.

In the negative "dar ánimos" is a sarcastic way of saying "I really appreciate your support".

Speaker A:

Te noto muy demacrado.

You look very wan.

Speaker B:

¡No me des ánimos!

Flattery will get you nowhere.

- Dar(le) atole con el dedo a - To feed gruel with your finger, To take advantage of someone's innocence

Sospecho que Carmen te está dando atole con el dedo. (I suspect Carmen is not playing fair with you.)

- Dar batería - To take sides; to be clear

Yo pagué la vez pasada; a ver si hoy das color. (I paid last time. It's your turn to pay.)

Ernesto no da color en el problema de la herencia. (Ernesto takes no sides in this business of the inheritance.)

Lalo, eres muy aguado. Ni pintas, ni das color. (Lalo, you're so wishy-washy. You can't decide one way or the other.)

- Dar(le) con la puerta en las narices a - To slam the door in someone's face (literally or figuratively)

Se enojó mucho y me dio con la puerta en las narices. (He got really upset and slammed the door in my face.)

- Dar(se) cuenta de;Dar(se) cuenta de que ... - To notice (that ...), To realize (that ...)

Me di cuenta del error demasiado tarde. (I noticed the mistake too late.)

¿No te das cuenta de que estás haciendo una tontería? (Don't you realize that what you're doing is not very bright?)

- Dar(le) cuerda a - To wind up, To egg on; to encourage; to humor

Rosendo siempre dice tonterías y Amalia siempre le da cuerda. (Rosendo always talks nonsense, and Amalia always eggs him on.)

¡Por amor de Dios, no le des cuerda! (For God's sake, don't encourage him!)

- Dar(se) cuerda solo(a) - To wind yourself up, To work yourself up, to get carried away

Desde que murió su mujer, Jorge se está dando cuerda solo. (Since his wife died, Jorge's been working himself into a real depression.)

- Dar(selas) de - To pretend to be you are not

Manuel se las da de arquitecto. (Manuel always passes himself off as an architect.)

- Dar de alta - To register; to sign up; to put on the payroll, etc.
  (except in a hospital, where dar de alta is to discharge a patient)

Si vas a trabajar, tienes que darte de alta en Hacienda. (If you're going to start working, you have to register as a taxpayer at the Treasury Department.)

Estas dos muchachas aún no están dadas de alta en la nueva escuela. (These two girls still haven't been registered at the new school.)

Ya llevo tres semanas trabajando aquí, y todavía no me dan de alta. (I've been working here for three weeks, and I still haven't been put on the payroll.)

Hijo, hay que dar de alta el coche nuevo. (Son, we have to register the new car.)

Doctor, ¿cuándo me dan de alta? Ya me quiero ir a casa. (Doctor, when will I be discharged from the hospital? I want to go home.)

- Dar de baja - To take off the registry, list, payroll, etc.

Me dieron de baja en el club cuando renuncié a la compañía. (When I quit my job, they cancelled my club membership.)

- Dar de botana - To put out to munch on

Nos dieron de botana aceitunas rellenas. (They gave us stuffed olives to munch on.)

- Dar de comer a - To feed

¿Ya le diste de comer a los niños? (Have the children eaten (been fed)?)

A esta hora siempre le da de comer al pollo. (She always feeds the chicken at this time.)

- Dar(se) el lujo de + verb - To give yourself the luxury of + verb, To be able to afford to + verb (not always connected with money)

No puedo darme el lujo de pelearme con mi jefe. (I can't afford to quarrel with my boss.)

- Dar(le) en la torre a - To hit on the tower, To do terrible to

Por confiado, ya te dieron en la torre. (You got taken because you're too trusting.)

- Dar(le) en qué pensar a - To give food for thought

Su actitud nos dio a todos mucho en qué pensar. (His attitude gave us all food for thought.)

- Dar ganas de (see Tener ganas) - To be appealing; to feel like

Con este calor dan ganas de meterse a nadar. (With this heat, you feel like getting into the pool.)

- Dar gato por liebre - To give a purchaser a cat instead of a hare, To deceive especially when referring to a purchase at the market.

No estoy seguro, pero creo que me dieron gato por liebre. (I'm not sure, but I think I was taken for a ride (I was deceived).)

- Dar(se) ínfulas (see Ser presumido) - To put on airs

Esa señora se da muchas ínfulas porque tiene título. (That woman puts on airs because she has a college degree.)

- Dar lástima (see Dar pena); Dar lata - To bother; to be a pain

Este coche da mucha lata. (This car is giving me a lot of trouble.)
La casera siempre está dando lata (es una latosa). (The landlady is always bugging me (she's a pain).)

- Dar mala espina - To give a bad thorn, To give a nasty feeling; to make suspicious

Su tardanza en resolver me da mala espina. (His delay in replying to my request makes me suspicious.)

- Dar patadas de ahogado - To thrash around uselessly in the water when you'll drown anyway, To fight a losing battle

Vicente, no pierdas el tiempo resistiéndote al divorcio. Son patadas de ahogado. (Vincent, don't waste your time trying to avoid the divorce. You're fighting a losing battle.)

- Dar pena; dar lástima - To (make) feel sorry for; To feel embarrassed; To take offense

Con tu modo de ser lograste que Irma te cortara; me das pena. (This is offensive; said in sympathy, this would be ¡Qué lástima! or ¡Qué pena!) (You are such a pain that Irma finally dropped you. I feel sorry for you.)
Me da pena pedirle dinero. (I feel embarrassed (I'm too timid) to ask her to lend me some money. Dar(se) por ofendido(a))
Hernán se dio por ofendido porque no aceptaron su propuesta. (Hernan took offense because his proposal was turned down.)

- Dar(le) por su lado a (see Seguirle la corriente a) - To humor, to go along with

Tu abuelo ya está viejo. No discutas con él. Dale por su lado para que no se enoje. (Your grandfather is old. Don't argue with him. Humor him so he doesn't get upset.)
Gloria le da por su lado a su marido para conservar la armonía. (Gloria goes along with everything her husband says just to keep the peace.)

- Dar(se) por vencido(a) - To give up

No he logrado conseguir suficiente dinero para el proyecto, pero me doy por vencido. (I haven't been able to raise all the money for the project, but I'm not giving up.)

- Dar(le) sabor al caldo - To give the broth some taste, To make things interesting

Las peripecias del viaje fueron las que le dieron sabor al caldo. (The unexpected things that happened on the trip were what made it interesting.)

- Dar trabajo (see Con trabajo(s) and Costar (mucho) trabajo) - To be difficult

Da mucho trabajo limpiar este piso. (It's a pain getting this floor clean.)

Easy Spanish Phrases

TRANSPORT

1.Where is the city hall? = ¿Dónde está el ayuntamiento?

2.The taxi stop is across the street = La parada de taxi está cruzando la calle.

3.Where is the bus stop? = ¿Dónde está la parada de autobús?

4.Could you please tell me where the main street is? = ¿Podría decirme dónde está la calle principal?

5.Is there a hotel nearby? = ¿Hay un hotel cerca?

6.Which way is downtown? = ¿Hacia dónde es el centro?

7.Should I turn right or left? = ¿Debo girar a la derecha o a la izquierda?

8.Is there a restaurant nearby? = ¿Hay un restaurante cerca?

9.How far is that place? = ¿Cómo de lejos está ese lugar?

10. Two streets more = Dos calles más.

11. Just a few metres from here = A sólo unos pocos metros de aquí.

12. You'll get there after passing the traffic lights = Llegarás allí después de pasar el semáforo.

13. On the next avenue = En la siguiente avenida.

14. On the opposite side = En el lado opuesto.

15. You need to get to the parallel street = Necesitas llegar a la calle paralela.

16. Keep going straight ahead = Siga recto.

17. There is an ATM to your left = Hay un cajero automático a tu izquierda.

18. Where can I find a pharmacy? = ¿Dónde puedo encontrar una farmacia?

19. The on-call pharmacy is near the community health center = La farmacia de guardia está cerca del ambulatorio.

20. Where is the nearest bakery? = ¿Dónde está la panadería más cercana?

21. The building is next to the park = El edificio está junto al parque.

22. There is a rest stop 200m from here = Hay una zona de ocio a 200 m de aquí.

23. What street are you looking for? = ¿Qué calle buscas?

24. Could you give me a reference site? = ¿Podrías darme un lugar de referencia?

25. Sorry, I don't know that place = Lo siento, no conozco ese lugar.

26. The name of the street sounds familiar = El nombre de la calle suena familiar.

27. I think I have been there = Creo que he estado allí.

28. I am not sure how to get there = No estoy seguro de cómo llegar.

29. Will you take me there? = ¿Me llevarías allí?

30. Are you sure it's that street? = ¿Estás seguro de que es esa calle?

31. Are you going there? = ¿Vas allí?

32. Should we go by car? = ¿Deberíamos ir en coche?

33. Should we go on foot? = ¿Deberíamos ir a pie?

34. Where is the train station? = ¿Dónde está la estación de tren?

35. How far is it from home? = ¿Cómo de lejos está de casa?

36. Where is the museum? = ¿Dónde está el museo?

37. Where is your friend's place? = ¿Dónde vive tu amigo?

38. Go past the roundabout = Pasa más allá de la rotonda.

39. You have to take a secondary road = Tienes que tomar una carretera secundaria.

40. Which way is faster to get there? = ¿Qué camino es más rápido para llegar allí?

41. Can you take me to the post office? = ¿Podrías llevarme a la oficina de correos?

42. I need to go home. Could you tell me how to go from here? = Necesito ir a casa, ¿podrías decirme cómo ir desde aquí?

43. How long does it take to get there? = ¿Cuánto se tarda en llegar allí?

44. Where is 5th Avenue? = ¿Dónde está la 5th Avenida?

45. Take the other road; this one is too bumpy = Toma la otra carretera; ésta tiene muchos baches.

46. Is there a bus that takes you to the hospital? = ¿Hay un autobús que te lleve al hospital?

47. How often can we find a bus stop along this street? = ¿Con qué frecuencia podemos encontrar una parada de bus a lo largo de esta calle?

48. I think it's not far from my place = Creo que no está lejos de mi casa.

49. Turn left when you reach the black building = Gira a la izquierda cuando llegues
al edificio negro.

50. The candy shop is next to the main square = La tienda de caramelos está junto a la plaza principal.

51. Turn right, left and right again, until you see a skyscraper = Gira a la derecha, izquierda y derecha de nuevo, hasta que veas un rascacielos.

52. Excuse me. Am I heading in the right direction to the old town area? = Disculpe, ¿voy en la dirección correcta para el casco antiguo?

53. Climb the stairs, you'll get there faster = Sube las escaleras, irás más rápido.

54. Go up to the last floor = Sube al último piso.

55. The medical practice is on the second floor = La consulta del médico está en la segunda planta.

56. You will find that office next to the elevator = Encontrarás esa oficina junto al ascensor.

57. Where is Ana's home? = ¿Dónde está la casa de Ana?

58. Where can I find public parking? = ¿Dónde puedo encontrar un aparcamiento público?

59. Is this restaurant close to a pub? = ¿Este restaurante está cerca de un pub?

60. You will find a quiet cove down that hill = Encontrarás una cala tranquila bajando esa colina.

61. Follow the signs to the main monuments = Sigue las señales para los monumentos principales.

62. Is this a pedestrian street? = ¿Ésta es una calle peatonal?

63. Is this a one way street? = ¿Ésta es una calle de sentido único?

64. Can I drive through that avenue? = ¿Puedo conducir por esa avenida?

65. Could you please tell me if I am near the university? = ¿Podría decirme si estoy cerca de la universidad, por favor?

66. How many streets should I cross? = ¿Cuántas calles debería cruzar?

67. Will I be able to get there in less than ten minutes? = ¿Podré llegar allí en menos de diez minutos?

68. You'll have to go to the other side of town = Tendrás que ir al otro lado de

la ciudad.

69. I don't know how to point the way = No sé cómo indicar el camino.

70. I could easily give directions = Podría dar indicaciones fácilmente.

71. I can point it out on a map = Puedo señalarlo en un mapa.

72. I am not sure how to get there = No estoy seguro de cómo llegar allí.

73. Could you tell me if this is the right way? = ¿Podrías decirme si éste es el camino correcto?

74. Where are we going? = ¿Dónde vamos?

75. This isn't the road I suggested = Ésta no es la carretera que sugerí.

76. Which way is the right to avoid traffic jams? = ¿Qué camino es el correcto para evitar atascos?

77. That street is longer, but safer = Esa calle es más larga, pero más segura.

78. I am totally lost = Estoy totalmente perdido.

79. Where are you going? = ¿Hacia dónde te diriges?

80. Is there any special place you want to see? = ¿Hay algún lugar en especial que quieras ver?

81. I need help to get somewhere = Necesito ayuda para llegar a un sitio.

82. Could you come with me? = ¿Podrías venir conmigo?

83. She walked me to the hotel = Ella me acompañó a pie hasta el hotel.

84. I would have never found the place myself = Yo nunca habría encontrado el sitio solo.

85. Those instructions helped me a lot = Esas instrucciones me ayudaron mucho.

86. Where is it in the map? = ¿Dónde está en el mapa?

87. Do you know this neighborhood? = ¿Conoces este barrio?

88. This is a dead-end street = Es una calle sin salida.

89. You should take this alley = Deberías tomar este pasaje.

90. Don't go that way, it is always crowded = No vayas por ahí, siempre está abarrotado.

91. You can take a shortcut here = Puedes tomar un atajo aquí.

92. The stairs will take you to the church = Las escaleras te llevarán a la iglesia.

93. How can I find a tattoo shop? = ¿Dónde puedo encontrar un estudio de tatuaje?

94. Excuse me, is this the ring road? = Disculpe, ¿es ésta la circunvalación?

95. How can I get to the fair? = ¿Cómo puedo llegar a la feria?

96. Should I go down that slope? = ¿Debería bajar esa pendiente?

97. Could you tell me where the bike path is? = ¿Podría decirme dónde está el carril bici?

98. Does this main highway go to the train station? = ¿Lleva esta carretera troncal a la estación de tren?

99. You must go straight ahead = Debes ir todo recto.

100.There is a wall, you will have to turn around = Hay un muro, tendrás que dar media vuelta.

TRAVEL

1. You will need to go through the park to get there faster = Necesitarás atravesar el parque para llegar allí más rápido.

2. The party is in the opposite way = La fiesta está en el sentido opuesto.

3. Should I go up or downhill? = ¿Debería subir o bajar la cuesta?

4. Can you take me to the local market? = ¿Podrías llevarme al mercado local?

5. After two roundabouts, turn right and continue fifty metres more = Después de dos rotondas, gira a la derecha y continúa cincuenta metros más.

6. Turn a corner = Girar en una esquina.

7. You can park on the street = Puedes aparcar en esta calle.

8. You can take either the ramp or the stairs = Puedes ir por la rampa o las escaleras.

9. You'll have to get the train there = Tendrás que tomar el tren para allá.

10. It is possible to go on foot, but it is far from here = Es posible llegar a pie, pero está lejos de aquí.

11. You should ask the police if you are lost = Deberías preguntar a la policía si estás perdido.

12. I'm going that way too = Yo también voy por ese camino.

13. It's tricky if you don't know the way = Es complicado si no conoces el camino.

14. Should we ask for directions now? = ¿Deberíamos pedir indicaciones ahora?

15. Are we going to the beach or the mountain? = ¿Vamos hacia la playa o la montaña?

16. Should we use the GPS? = ¿Deberíamos usar el GPS?

18. We better take a look at the signs = Mejor echamos un vistazo a las señales.

19. There is a crossing at the end of the street = Hay un cruce al final de la calle.

20. You should turn left and then right at the next corner = Deberías girar a la izquierda y después a la derecha en la siguiente esquina.

21. How many metres are there between your house and the park? = ¿Cuántos metros hay entre tu casa y el parque?

22. Which way? Through that narrow alley? = ¿Por dónde? ¿Atravesando ese callejón estrecho?

23. You should take that road, it's new = Deberías ir por esa carretera, es nueva.

24. If you follow the marked path, you'll get to the cabin = Si sigues el camino señalado, llegarás a la cabaña.

25. The hiking trail starts from that sign = La pista de senderismo comienza desde esa señal.

26. We have this new bike trail = Tenemos esta nueva pista para ciclismo.

27. The guide will give you good directions = El guía te dará buenas indicaciones.

28. How many different ways are there to get to that place? = ¿Cuántos caminos diferentes hay para llegar a ese sitio?

29. Do night buses stop here? = ¿Paran aquí los autobuses nocturnos?

30. Where should I go for information on local events? = ¿Dónde debería ir para obtener información sobre eventos locales?

31. This avenue goes across the whole village = Esta avenida cruza todo el pueblo.

32. How can I get to the airport? = ¿Cómo puedo llegar al aeropuerto?

33. This street leads to my office = Esta calle lleva a mi oficina.

34. You will find that shop two blocks from here = Encontrarás esa tienda a dos calles de aquí.

35. The butcher is around the corner = La carnicería está al girar la esquina.

36. How many floors do I have to go up? = ¿Cuántas plantas tengo que subir?

37. Where is the service entrance? = ¿Dónde está la entrada de servicio?

38. Can you tell me the way out? = ¿Podría indicarme la salida?

39. How can I get to the town from here? = ¿Cómo podría llegar al ayuntamiento desde aquí?

40. Could you tell me the meaning of those signs? = ¿Podría decirme el significado de esas señales?

41. Can you tell me where the gas station is from here? = Iré desde aquí, ¿podrías decirme dónde está la gasolinera?

42. You will see the path clearly from the top of that hill = Verás el camino con claridad desde arriba de esa colina.

43. You will find the consignment for your luggage in that hall = Encontrarás la consigna para tu equipaje en esa sala.

44. Could you tell me where the restroom is, please? = ¿Podría decirme dónde está el aseo, por favor? 45. How can I get to the claims office? = ¿Cómo llego a la oficina de reclamaciones?

46. Follow those lights to the boarding gate = Sigue esas luces hasta la puerta de embarque.

47. Down and to the right = Al fondo a la derecha.

48. You will get to the unemployment line after turning that corner = Llegarás a la línea del paro después de girar esa esquina.

49. You can use this huge building as a landmark = Puedes tomar este enorme edificio como punto de referencia.

50. This bank is the first of a line that will take you to the end of the square = Este banco es el primero de una línea que te llevará al final de la plaza.

51. Take the train here and get off after three stops = Toma el tren aquí y baja después de tres paradas.

SHOPPING

1. Excuse me, do you have this shirt in a smaller size? = Disculpe, ¿tiene esta camisa en una talla más pequeña?

2. Could you tell me the price of this item? = ¿Podría decirme el precio de este artículo?

3. Where can I find a shoe shop? = ¿Dónde puedo encontrar una zapatería?

4. Can I have a refund? = ¿Puedo obtener un reembolso?

5. Is it possible to try this at home? = ¿Es posible probar esto en casa?

6. Is there a shopping center in this town? = ¿Hay un centro comercial en esta ciudad?

7. Is the shop open on weekends? = ¿Abre la tienda los fines de semana?

8. What hours do you work? = ¿Cuál es tu horario de trabajo?

9. Does this suit me? = ¿Me queda bien esto?

10. Do you have this in a different color? = ¿Tiene esto en un color diferente?

11. Can I pay in dollars? = ¿Puedo pagar en dólares?

12. Where can I find a local shop to buy some souvenirs? = ¿Dónde puedo encontrar una tienda local
para comprar algunos recuerdos?

13. How much is that in pounds? = ¿Cuánto es eso en libras?

14. Which size is a Spanish M? = ¿Qué talla es una M española?

15. What is the name of a shop where you buy fish? = ¿Cuál es el nombre de una tienda donde compras pescado?

16. Is this a 24/7 store? = ¿Es esta una tienda 24h?

17. Can I buy sheets here? = ¿Puedo comprar sábanas aquí?

18. What exactly do you sell? = ¿Qué vendes exactamente?

19. Is this a second hand shop? = ¿Es esta una tienda de segunda mano?

20. Is this a bargain shop? = ¿Es esta una tienda de oportunidades?

21. Do you sell seasonal fruit? = ¿Vende fruta de temporada?

22. Do you sell typical regional food? = ¿Vende comida típica de la región?

23. Do your products have a certificate of origin? = ¿Sus productos tienen denominación de origen?

24. What are you buying? = ¿Qué compras?

25. How much are you planning to spend? = ¿Cuánto planeas gastar?

26. What do you need from here? = ¿Qué necesitas de aquí?

27. Is this food properly canned? = ¿Está envasada adecuadamente esta comida?

28. Where can I find a gourmet shop? = ¿Dónde puedo encontrar una tienda gourmet?

29. Will I get a refund? = ¿Obtendré un reembolso?

30. Can I exchange this for another item? = ¿Puedo cambiarlo por otro artículo?

31. Could you gift wrap it? = ¿Podría envolverlo para regalo?

32. Do you have something for a newborn? = ¿Tiene algo para un recién nacido?

33. Do you have wedding registry here? = ¿Tienen listas de boda aquí?

34. Do you offer gift certificates? = ¿Ofrecen certificados de regalo?

35. Is it possible to order something that is not in the shop now? = ¿Es posible pedir algo que no está en la tienda ahora?

36. When will you have it? = ¿Cuándo lo tendrá?

37. Do you also repair clothes? = ¿También hacen arreglos de ropa?

38. What do you need to buy? = ¿qué necesitas comprar?

39. I would like to visit some boutiques = Me gustaría visitar algunas boutiques.

40. This was the first shop in town = Ésta fue la primera tienda en la ciudad.

41. The old town is full of charming little shops = El casco antiguo está lleno de encantadoras tiendecitas. 42. This is a luxury furniture shop = Ésta es una tienda de muebles de lujo.

43. People from other towns come to this huge shopping centre = Gente de otras ciudades viene a este enorme centro comercial.

44. Does this business comply with the regulations? = ¿Cumple la normativa esta tienda?

45. They sell many odd items here = Aquí venden muchos artículos curiosos.

46. Where can I buy some art supplies? = ¿Dónde puedo comprar algo de material para manualidades? 47. I will take a final look at the local shops = Echaré un último vistazo a las tiendas locales.

48. I always come back with something from the duty free zone = Siempre vuelvo con algo de la zona libre de impuestos.

49. This is a wonderful haberdashery (clothier) store! = ¡Esta mercería es genial!

50. I'm looking for a herbalist's shop = Busco una herboristería.

51. Is there any place near to buy ground coffee? = ¿Hay algún lugar cerca para comprar café molido? 52. They have freshly baked bread here = Aquí tienen pan recién hecho.

53. They sell all types of tea in this shop = Venden todo tipo de té en esta tienda.

54. This is a barter spot = Éste es un lugar de trueque.

55. They sell things on consignment = Venden cosas en consigna.

56. You can bring your old clothes to this second hand shop = Puedes traer tu ropa vieja a esta tienda de segunda mano.

57. Do you accept credit cards? = ¿Acepta tarjetas de crédito?

58. I will pay in cash, thank you = Pagaré en efectivo, gracias.

59. I will need an invoice for my boss = Necesitaré una factura para mi jefe.

60. You have two weeks to exchange the item = Tiene dos semanas para cambiar el artículo.

61. Which material is this made of? = ¿De qué material está hecho ésto?

62. Is this real leather? = ¿Es cuero verdadero?

63. Is this synthetic? = ¿Es sintético?

64. Is this pure cotton? = ¿Es algodón puro?

65. What kind of dye do you use? = ¿Qué clase de tinte usas?

66. Is this hypoallergenic? = ¿Es hipoalergénico?

67. Do you have this for other ages? = ¿Tiene ésto para otras edades? 68.How many of these do you have? = ¿Cuántos de éstos tiene? 69.What does this shop offer? = ¿Qué ofrece esta tienda?

70. I will need more = Necesitaré más.

71. Are you open on weekends? = ¿Abre los fines de semana?

72. Is this shop part of a chain? = ¿Esta tienda es parte de una cadena?

73. Does this supermarket sell local products? = ¿Vende este supermercado productos locales?

74. Is this organic food? = ¿Es comida ecológica?

75. What is the price range? = ¿Cuál es el rango de precios?

76. They have a wide selection of footwear here = Aquí tienen una amplia selección de calzado.

77. How many businesses are there in this shopping center? = ¿Cuántos negocios hay en este centro comercial?

78. Do you sell food for gluten intolerant people? = ¿Venden comida para gente intolerante al gluten? 79. Where do your products come from? = ¿De dónde vienen sus productos?

80. Do you have this in stock? = ¿Tiene existencias de ésto?

81. How many chairs go with this table? = ¿Cuántas sillas van con esta mesa?

82. This product is out of stock = Este producto está agotado.

83. I'm looking for an unlisted item = Busco un artículo descatalogado.

84. Do you have an online shop? = ¿Tiene tienda en línea?

85. Do you offer DIY kits? = ¿Ofrecen kits para aficionados?

86. Is there currently any additional offer? = ¿Actualmente hay alguna oferta adicional?

87. I was looking for a special gift = Buscaba un regalo especial.

88. Could you tell me about this piece of art? = ¿Podría hablarme sobre esta obra de arte?

89. Do you offer party kits for children? = ¿Ofrecen kits de fiesta para niños?

90. Do you make deliveries overseas? = ¿Hacen envíos al extranjero?

91. If I buy this here, could I receive it back home? = Si compro ésto aquí, ¿podría recibirlo en casa?

92. Is this handmade? = ¿Está hecho a mano?

93. Is it possible to finance these products? = ¿Es posible financiar estos productos?

94. Do I have to make a down payment? = ¿Tengo que dejar un depósito?

95. Which is the latest model? = ¿Cuál es el último modelo?

96. I would need to know the product specifications = Necesitaría saber las especificaciones del producto.

97. Is this made of natural fibers? = ¿Está hecho de fibras naturales?

98. Is this battery-operated? = ¿Funciona con batería?

99. What is the lifespan of this printer? = ¿Cuál es la vida útil de esta impresora?

100. Are the batteries included? = ¿Están incluidas las pilas?

101. Is this suitable for babies? = ¿Es adecuado para bebés?

102 .Is this ready to use? = ¿Está listo para usar?

103. Is this an exclusive design? = ¿Es un diseño exclusivo?

104. Do you have more products from this manufacturer? = ¿Tiene más

productos de este fabricante? 105. Do you sell vintage items? = ¿Vende artículos vintage?

106. Do you collaborate with other brands? = ¿Colaboran con otras marcas?

107. Is this your only shop in the town? = ¿Es su única tienda en la ciudad?

108. Excuse me, I have some questions = Disculpe, tengo algunas preguntas.

109. Sorry, I need to check with my family first = Lo siento, necesito consultar a mi familia primero.

110. Are these for beginners? = ¿Son para principiantes?

111. Do you have any computer manuals? = ¿Tiene manuales informáticos?

112. Do you offer installation services? = ¿Ofrecen servicios de instalación?

113. How much is it to ship it to my home? = ¿Cuánto cuesta recibirlo en casa?

114. Could we set an appointment to design the products? = ¿Podríamos fijar una cita para diseñar los productos?

115. There is always a line here; you'll have to wait = Siempre hay cola aquí, tendréis que esperar.

116. This bar opens twice a week = Este bar abre dos veces por semana.

117. We close for the public when we host a party = Cerramos al público cuando damos una fiesta.

118. You can buy kitchen utensils here = Puedes comprar utensilios de cocina aquí.

119. How much is it to rent an inflatable castle? = ¿Cuánto cuesta alquilar un castillo hinchable?

120. Every business along this avenue is fashion related = Cada negocio de esta avenida está relacionado con la moda.

121.You will find top brands at deep discounts = Encontrarás primeras marcas con grandes descuentos.

CONCLUSION

(CONCLUSIÓN)

Learning a second language is not that easy but you have to admit that it is challenging. Aside from your native language, it is quite challenging to learn about a very unfamiliar language like the Spanish Language. *(Aprender un segundo idioma no es tan fácil, pero debes admitir que es un desafío. Además de su idioma nativo, es bastante difícil aprender sobre un idioma muy desconocido como el español.)*

Here, you have learned the correct pronunciation of some Spanish words, the proper gestures that must accompany the statement that you are making, and also the use of verbs, pronouns, nouns, adjectives, adverbs, prepositions and the like. Through this tool, you have learned all grammatical factors without enrolling in a formal class-type review of Spanish Language. *(Aquí, ha aprendido la pronunciación correcta de algunas palabras en español, los gestos adecuados que deben acompañar a la declaración que está haciendo, y también el uso de verbos, pronombres, sustantivos, adjetivos, adverbios, preposiciones y similares. A través de esta herramienta, ha aprendido todos los factores gramaticales sin inscribirse en una revisión formal de clase de español.)*

Furthermore, there are also short stories which make the learning even more exciting. Through some tips in reading, you will surely find Spanish Language reading and learning enjoyable instead of considering it as a burden. (Además, también hay historias cortas que hacen que el aprendizaje sea aún más emocionante. A través de algunos consejos en lectura, seguramente encontrará agradable la lectura y el aprendizaje del idioma español en lugar de considerarlo como una carga.)

The use of short stories may be considered as designed for kids or children who are learning through baby steps, but the truth is that a learner of second language is considered as baby steps too. There is no harm in considering it as a kid-like way of learning. That is again a form of humility. Remember that humility is the start of learning. *(El uso de cuentos cortos puede considerarse diseñado para niños o niños que están aprendiendo a través de pequeños pasos, pero la verdad es que un aprendiz de segundo idioma también se considera como pequeños pasos. No hay daño en considerarlo como una forma de aprendizaje infantil. Esa es nuevamente una forma de humildad. Recuerda que la humildad es el comienzo del aprendizaje.)*

As parting words, you should always carve in your mind that learning is one way of showing humility because you are admitting into yourself that you still have a lot to learn and that will make you even more fit to perfect your goal – in this instance, the Spanish Language and Grammar. *(Como palabras de despedida, siempre debes recordar que aprender es una forma de mostrar humildad porque admites en ti mismo que todavía tienes mucho que aprender y que te hará aún más apto para perfeccionar tu objetivo; en este caso, Lengua y gramática española.)*

CPSIA information can be obtained
at www.ICGtesting.com
Printed in the USA
BVHW050757120521
607047BV00003B/528